Scriptures marked THE VOI(
Voice): Scripture taken from
Ecclesia Bible Society. Used by

MW00574866

All emphasis within Scripture quotations is the author's own.

Cover design by Robert Connor

Edited by Jane E. Infante

ISBN: 978-1-948680-95-0

Endorsement

Doc Scott and I have known each other for several years now and I count him as one of my friends. We've had some wonderful ministry times together as well as great personal times of fellowship. I can truly say that in "Chain Breakers", you get the benefit of things the Lord has revealed to him as well as the personal real-life situations that give validation to the revelation he shares. The wisdom and understanding presented holds a key for many to finally break the chains that free you to walk in who you really are in Christ, just the way He designed it. It's time to break that cycle of shame and cast off those shackles! I highly recommend this devotional by Dr. Scott Infante. You will be beyond blessed.... You will be FREE!

Michael Van Vlymen
Author and Speaker
www.riverofblessingsinternationalministries.org/

Dedication

I dedicate this devotional book to my wife, Jane—the love of my life, who is my life partner and power ally. In all things, at the end of the day, every day, we are best friends doing life and ministry together as we walk hand in hand with Jesus.

Table of Contents

Foreword 1

Preface 3

Acknowledgments 7

Day 1 – Why Shame? 9

Day 2 – Defining Shame 13

Day 3 – Origins of Shame 17

Day 4 – Naked and Unashamed 23

Day 5 – Shame, Contempt and Violence 29

Day 6 – Two Prostitutes 35

Day 7 – A Room Divided 41

Day 8 – Silencing the Voice of the Enemy 47

Day 9 – You Are Not Your DNA 53

Day 10 – You Manifest What You Believe 59

Day 11 – Love Wins 65

Day 12 – Lost in Yonkers 73

Day 13 – Sickness Minus Shame 77

Day 14 – Shame in Disappointment 83

Day 15 – Shame Makes Us Run 89

Day 16 – Quick Trip Back to the Garden 95

Day 17 – Modern Day Prodigals 103

Day 18 – The Faith of a Child 109

Day 19 – Baptism and the God that Answers by Fire 115

Day 20 – Orphan Dream 121

Day 21 – Shame and the Law 127

Day 22 – *Destiny Destroys Shame* *133*

Day 23 – *Freedom from the Voice of Saul* *139*

Day 24 – *Positioned in Unshakable Grace* *147*

Day 25 – *Prayer for Breaking Trauma Over Our Bodies
         and Releasing Resurrection* *155*

Day 26 – *Revolution of Love* *163*

Day 27 – *The Restoration of Men and Women* *169*

Day 28 – *Freedom from Regret* *179*

Day 29 – *Sight Restored* *185*

Day 30 – *The Father's Blessing* *191*

Afterword *199*

About the Author *201*

Foreword

This thirty-day devotional will help you unmask the hidden shame that is holding back your God ordained destiny. Once the shame comes out into the light, God will shatter the prison walls and open the doors to LIBERTY through repentance, the cleansing of the Word, and the Holy Spirit's revelation on how much you are loved by God! You must be free of every vestige of shame to participate in the GREATER GLORY OF GOD.

Dr. Scott Infante makes it easy with his 30-Day Devotional, "Chain Breakers". Thirty days of the Word and Holy Spirit heart revelation build faith to set you free to be a world changer! As you are free, you will become a Glory carrier for the greatest outpouring of God's Spirit in history. I call it the season of the Greater Glory.

In the past, revivals have all dwindled and come to an end and things went back to normal. This move will not only not end until Jesus returns — in fact, it will keep on increasing! Read about it in Ezekiel 47. It will be like the water that flowed from the Temple. It started with a trickle and became a river that could only be navigated by swimming. And wherever the river went, there would be life!

This is what we are entering into on planet earth! Your greatest days are ahead of you.

"For the Glory of the Lord rises to shine on you, Darkness as black as night covers all the nations of the earth, but the Glory of the Lord rises and appears over you. All nations will come to your light; mighty kings will come to see your radiance."

-Isaiah 60:2, 3 (New Living Translation)

1

Blessings and Greater Glory,

Sid Israel Roth
Host, It's Supernatural!

Preface

This is no ordinary devotional. It's not warm fuzzy reading that makes you feel good but gritty, sometimes raw, stories that expose the core of shame. Shame is that pervasive feeling that I am deeply flawed that doesn't go away, or if it does, it is only for a fleeting moment. The goal of this devotional is to paint a picture of what shame looks like and what the Holy Spirit's transformational work looks like as He crafts us into who we were always meant to be.

At the end of each day in this 30-Day devotional is a prayer to engage with and a daily declaration for you declare. Many days are encounter-based as you walk hand-in-hand with Holy Spirit in your journey to transformation. As you engage with the stories which are both personal and biblical, the truth of God's word will break you free from the chains of shame. You will encounter the God of the Universe who is ravenously jealous to meet with you and to own your heart.

This is no ordinary devotional. There are not many out there that are built around the concept of *shame*. Personally, when I think of a devotional, I tend to think of warm, fuzzy reading that makes me feel good. Something inspirational to start the day—NOT gritty, sometimes raw, stories that expose the core of my shame. Nonetheless, I have to go with what's in me—something that looks the source of much of our pain right in the eye, something that brings healing and freedom in the place of this greatest of culprits. Shame. Shame is that pervasive feeling that we are deeply flawed that doesn't go away, or if it does, it remains lurking in the shadows.

A number of years ago, I went back to school to get my doctoral degree in education. True to form, when deciding on a topic for my dissertation, I didn't opt for something conventional like the comparison between "Reading Program A" and "Reading Program B." I asked the Lord for a topic that really mattered, a study that could have an impact on current and upcoming generations.

It has long been my passion to be a part of the healing and launching of generations — generations that I have had the privilege to teach and father over the years. What He led me to was the study of the detrimental effects of pornography psychologically, physically (like the brain), and spiritually. No shame there, right?! My paper, *A Systematic Review of the Physiological, Psychological, and Spiritual Impact of Pornography in Males*, sought to highlight some of the areas of deepest bondage in Christendom today.

As a high school teacher, I have stood in the midst of the most pornified generation to date in my classroom and I have been keenly aware of the enemy's plan to obliterate a generation's capacity to love through their bondage to the false presence of an image on a screen. I also know that God uses the "least of these" and those things that are foolish to the world to demonstrate His glory to all creation. God has a strategy to thwart the enemy's plan by raising up a generation of dread champions who walk in unparalleled anointing and power. Their areas of weakness will be turned into strength as He brings the power of His redemption. They will be a generation that ushers in the greatest Love Revolution the world has ever known.

The Lord told me that shame is the culprit that has undergirded every addiction and form of modern idolatry and that unmasking shame is key to breaking the chains that keep His people addicted.

Shame is what keeps them tethered to the lie that a gulf of separation exists between them and God. Jesus came to remove that separation. In fact, it was obliterated on the cross. Once we truly understand and accept that, shame has no more hold.

To be brutally honest, writing this devotional began very slowly. I was hit hard with devil's lie that I had nothing worthwhile to say. Simultaneously, as it is whenever we endeavor to bring others into that which we have received from the Lord, my shame issues were slapping me in the face left and right. Of course, they were—the enemy of my soul was rattled because he knows the power of shame to keep us bound in self-destructive patterns of behaving and relating. That's why I did this devotional series.

This book is centered around facilitating an encounter between you and the One who made you. My goal in this devotional is to paint a picture of what shame looks like and what the transformational work of the Holy Spirit looks like as He crafts us into the people we were always meant to be. At the end of each day in this 30-Day devotional is a prayer that I invited you to pray with me and declare as many times as you need in your journey to manifest what you believe and Who you behold.

My hope is that the words on these pages provoke your conversation with God in ways that foster a greater intimacy with Him—that's what I believe a good devotional should do. My prayer is that, as you engage with the stories which are both personal and biblical, the truth of God's word is married in your heart to an encounter with the Holy Spirit that renews your hope on the journey and that brings great freedom as you encounter the God of the Universe who is ravenously jealous to meet you and to own your heart.

If you're interested in a more in-depth program, the course we developed under the same name will be a good resource for you.

Blessings,

Doc Scott

Acknowledgments

First and foremost, I thank God for His enduring grace and love that enabled me not only to write, but to experience tangible grace as my own shame got triggered repeatedly in the process. One cannot write about shame without encountering it.

My wife, Jane, is a writer and artist in her own right, which makes "editor" an inadequate term, one that does not do justice in describing the gift she carries. This book is the product of two wordsmiths who have both endeavored to craft language that may be unfamiliar to some into something that is tangible and accessible for many. This is certainly our prayer.

This work has also been influenced by the gifts and wealth of knowledge and experience of other friends, authors and ministers who I love and deeply admire.

I'd like to extend a huge thanks to Sid Roth for believing in me and supporting this project!

Heartfelt thanks to my friend and mentor, Michael Van Vlymen. He articulates the Christian concept of the "sanctified imagination" as the bridge to the supernatural and has greatly influenced the way I access God.

I owe a debt of gratitude to Christopher P. Carter, who makes encountering God via our imagination simple—which is what it is supposed to be.

A huge thank you to my parents for supporting me as I got my doctorate--of which this book is an outgrowth.

I would be remiss to not acknowledge friends who have walked through many fires with us while consistently mining the gold in our hearts and calling us forth into all that God has for us. Karla Lopez and Juliette Quoquoi, who are family in the truest sense of the word, and our online community, Hammer School of the Prophets, are the community who has stood behind us and cheered us on in every way. My wife and I would not be who we are today without them. With all my heart, thank you!!

DAY 1

Why Shame?

"I sometimes think that shame, mere awkward, senseless shame, does as much toward preventing good acts and straightforward happiness as any of our vices can do."

-C.S. LEWIS, A GRIEF OBSERVED[1]

Some of my best worship time is in the shower. For me, the shower and the car are my sanctuaries. When I am in either, it is often the only time I am not distracted by a million other things. I have had to redefine what it means to have a "quiet time" in the context of simply doing life. Not that I don't have other time to sit down and read the Word and do things like journaling. But my worship and processing time tends to be in the shower and the car. My son—an amazing African American young man—wanted to turn me on to a couple of new worship artists to add to my shower list. I listened to the first song on the playlist that he made for me, and I thought, "Wow, this is great." I loved how the black artist took a typical worship song on the first track and crafted it into an encounter with God in the layered harmonies and vocal runs. I was not remotely prepared for what came next, and I nearly came

---

[1] Lewis, C S. A Grief Observed. London: Faber & Faber, 1968.

unhinged emotionally when I heard the words in Johnathan McReynolds' song, "Cycles."[2]
It said,

> *"Didn't I conquer this last year?*
> *Tell me what I missed 'cause I fear*
> *That it's coming back up again...*
> *The devil wants to extend the game, free throws*
> *And when it ends he wants to make the sequel...*
> *See the devil, he learns from your mistakes*
> *Even if you don't.*
> *That's how he keeps you in cycles, cycles..."*

The first stanza caught my attention because it was not the type of language you heard in a worship song at church on Sunday. I knew I liked it already because it was not religious. The second verse stole my breath and brought tears to my eyes as I wrapped my head around the fact that he was talking about destructive cycles and how the devil "...learns from your mistakes, even if you don't."

An epiphany is like a sledge-hammer to the psyche, and this epiphany clobbered me between the eyes. The meaning exploded in my mind, and I became suddenly and excruciatingly aware that one of the enemy's weapons of war is making freedom the proverbial carrot stick that we never can attain. Why? Because we are embroiled in "cycles"—mindsets, habits, recurring emotional roadblocks, paralyzing self-contempt, and relational impasses that never find their resolve

---

[2] McReynolds, J. (2018). "Cycles." Make Room. Light Records, Entertainment One Music. (Cycles lyrics © All Essential Music, Capitol Cmg Genesis, United Pursuit Music)

in our Christian liberty.

When I was praying about beginning this devotional, the Lord emblazoned a thought on my heart. He said, "If you unmask and deconstruct shame, you will destroy the very foundation upon which every addiction and form of idolatry is built."

I wrote my doctoral dissertation on the psychological, physiological (brain), and spiritual effects of pornography on males[3], because I have been radically confronted with the pornification of a generation. Porn has become mainstream, and the stigma surrounding its use has diminished in our media culture. Yet, I never came across a study in my research literature review that addressed the monolith of shame embedded in the hearts of every individual since the Garden and fall of man.

I knew what the Lord was saying was intrinsically right—that shame was lodged in the bedrock of the human heart. I did not know what that really meant and even more so how to "unmask" or "deconstruct" it. But I sensed Holy Spirit's invitation to launch out, to move away from shore and see where He takes us. This 30-day devotional is a journey I'm taking together with you—and I trust it will be an authentic and radically transformational one for us all. So, I dare you to jump in with both feet as we travel together. I am profoundly aware God will meet us because it is what He does, like a good Father who is always (present continuous) pursuing His children.

---

[3] Infante, S. (2018). A Systematic Review of the Psychological, Physiological, & Spiritual Effects of Pornography on Males. [Trevecca Nazarene University]. Proquest Dissertations and Theses Global. See link: https://www.proquest.com/docview/2176080401/DF19C52B56454278PQ/19

Pray this with me:

Father, I do not fully know what shame is and how it impacts my relationship to myself, others, and, more importantly, to You. But (deep breath) I am all in. I want to know what it means to be entirely vulnerable, "naked," and unashamed before You. I want to feel at home in my own skin. I want to be awakened and fully alive as a human without fear, without condemnation, without self-destructive cycles that keep me embroiled in the struggle. I am laying down trying to manage my life and "get it right" independently. Engage me, encounter me, and make me into a man or woman that gives You glory. I, the created, look to You as my Creator and say, "I'm Yours," in Jesus' Name. Amen.

DAY 2

Defining Shame

"Shame is internalized when one is abandoned. Abandonment is the precise term to describe how one loses one's authentic self and ceases to exist psychologically."

-JOHN BRADSHAW [4]

S hame can seem nebulous to define, but it is easy to paint a picture of what it looks and feels like. When I was five years old, my biological father (Gary) walked out the door and never returned. As a teen and young adult, I rationalized his abandonment, saying that it was just about him "chasing a skirt," which was true. But that shallow explanation never did one thing to heal the cavern in my heart.

Thankfully, children are resilient in many ways, and they tend to keep going regardless of what has happened. On the outside, it is sometimes hard to see the damage on the inside. Later, their behavior and emotional life may betray them as that which was entombed in the heart starts to crack and begins to seep out, sometimes in a trickle over time or other times, busting through like a dam that breaks wide open

---

[4] Bradshaw, J. (2015). Healing the shame that binds you. Health Communications.

without warning.

I remember coming home one day with mom, and our front door was unhinged, and the scene on the inside looked like a tornado had just blown through, tossing everything into random places in the house and leaving in a hurry. My mom burst into tears while she called the police and attempted to make sense of this reckless, senseless robbery. Across the room, on the terrazzo floor, I spotted a Big Wheel that my mother's boss had come over and assembled on a lunch break.

Mom nodded her okay for me to go and ride my new unspoiled toy, which served to usher me from the shambles into the haven of a child's world on the other side of the door. Like many children, when their world has been blown to smithereens, I rode my Big Wheel with abandon, carrying the shrapnel of an obliterated, dismantled world in my heart.

When my dad left us, something deep and penetrating lodged itself in the hard drive of my heart to continually run in the background, informing my emotions, responses to future abandonment, abuse, rejections, and seeming deprivations. The young adult could rationalize, but children do not. They are ego-centric. They interpret everything that happens in the house that creates discord, tension, and distress as something about them. The five-year-old in me didn't blame an adulterous affair but said in his heart, "What's wrong with me that Daddy doesn't love me anymore?" That is what shame looks like.

Shame says, "I am not enough; I am wrong, defective, the one to blame. I am unwanted and unlovable." Many children of dysfunctional families are familiar with the roles they played in the family in their attempt to fix the problem. Some become a confidant to a parent; some become the clown and comic relief. Others rebel, making them the black sheep and the one their parents identify as "the problem" instead of their own [the parents'] behavior.

The seedbed for all types of mental illness is early wounding that creates a wasteland of the heart. Self-protective boundaries forged in the heart to avoid death or what feels like death make the heart immovable, inflexible and impervious to change. This is where personality disorders which are pervasive in their impact on the personality are created. Only a heart that remains flexible, embraces change, and eventually dislodges the stony places through forgiveness and the cleansing blood of Jesus is free to be truly unencumbered to love.

Jesus said, "Let the little children come to me, and do not hinder them, for the kingdom of heaven belongs to such as these" (*New International Version*, Matt. 19:4). Jesus bids every child inside the man and woman to come to Him. There is no such thing as re-parenting in the literal earthly sense. We can never go backwards in our flesh and get what we did not get from our parents.

We have only one Parent, and He has a Name—it's Jesus. God may use fathers and mothers of faith as agents of healing, but the deep caverns of need belong to Him alone to fill. The good news is that Jesus never just fills and heals. He does exceedingly above and beyond all that we can imagine. He is the Redeemer who inhabits our weakness and pours His glory into it; He works all things together for good—redeeming all. He doesn't just fix us; He liberates us to love and to be agents of healing to the world.

Pray this with me:

Father, I, the created, look to You, the Creator, to tell me who I am. For everything in me, everything that I have done, everything that others have done to me that I have given the power to name me, I repent. I forgive those whose actions left me feeling like I was not good enough, not lovable enough, unwanted, or just plain defective. I forgive myself for the places I have held myself hostage to an unreachable, unattainable standard. Forgive me for every attempt I have made to fix myself, identify myself falsely by pumping myself up, or degrading those around me to make me feel better. I declare, even with trepidation, that You alone have the power to tell me who I am. You alone own the rights to my soul, my DNA, heart, and mind.

Everywhere that I have felt abandoned and rejected by others through their intentionality or my perception of their motivation, I invite You to fill me and inscribe Your words of identity on the hard drive of my heart.

I choose to cast off the veil of shame that has enveloped me. I ask You to permeate my soul with Your righteousness as You make all things right, and Your completeness, as You convince my heart I am enough in You, lifting my head, liberating me to be vulnerable and naked before You, even now. Show me where You were in the times of hurt and trauma, let me see You entering those hurtful memories and bringing Your perspective and Your Presence (stop now and let Him show you. Invite Him into those places and see what He does). Let me hear Your Voice speaking to the little child in me. Heal me and make me whole. In Jesus' Name. Amen.

DAY 3

Origins of Shame

'God called to the Man: "Where are you?" He said,
"I heard you in the garden, and I was afraid
because I was naked. And I hid."'

-THE MESSAGE, GEN. 3:9-10

hen my oldest daughter, Sarah, was five years old and
we were saying our bedtime prayers, I said, "Thank
you, Lord, that we are created in Your image." Sarah, in her
childlike attentiveness, looked up at me and said, "Daddy, what
does it mean to be created in God's image?" I was stumped, and
my face showed how discombobulated I was as my thoughts
raced on how to articulate such a profound concept to a five-
year-old. I used this kind of language to talk about our identity
because, as a pastor, I had conducted many conferences that
touched on issues of identity and healing.

After a few minutes, I blurted my honest response and
said, "I don't really know, honey, but it's kinda like God put a
huge stamp of Himself on the inside of you and me, and it's
always there, because we are His." I am sure that cleared things
up for her! There is something good about the way little girls
are enamored with their fathers. They often let us dads off the
hook, which she did by her quick agreement with my
explanation without any follow-up questions.

Unbeknownst to her, she covered my shame with the
look in her eyes that said I was "enough" for her at that moment

and, beyond being enough—I was adored. To feel loved and cherished by the people we love the most and risk being so vulnerable before them is overwhelming and profoundly impacting.

Adam had an unfettered, adoring relationship with God in the Garden—one that anchored him, secured his soul. Then, suddenly, unexpectedly, in one act of disobedience, he found himself painfully aware that he was naked, self-conscious, ravaged of innocence—so he hid. Self-consciousness is the doorway to the disease of introspection—that excruciating, debasing, critical inward-looking that we do in our descent into the "hell of self." Chambered in our personal hell, we are held captivate by our self-contempt, which is not ransomed easily. After the Fall, the Genesis account tells us that when Adam and Eve heard God walking in the garden, "God called to the man, 'Where are you?' He said, 'I heard you in the garden, and I was afraid because I was naked. And I hid" (MSG, Gen. 3: 9-10).

Hiding is a shame response. Hiding in shame is when we emotionally or even sometimes physically go away, isolate ourselves, attempt to crawl under a rock, or cover ourselves in anything that diverts the attention away from sudden exposure. I find it interesting that Adam did not hide because he did something wrong. He hid because he felt utterly unhinged in his sense of inadequacy, wrongness, and unfamiliar nakedness.

The churched response to the question, "Why did Adam hide?" would be "because he did something bad." But Adam did not say that he hid because he ate from the Tree of the Knowledge of Good and Evil. He said he hid because he was naked.

Being found out for doing something wrong was not Adam's fear, but rather he feared that he was exposed as "being" something bad, rotten to the core. Doing something terrible relates to guilt. Guilt is different from shame in that the resolution of guilt has freedom as its goal. Once owned and confessed, wrongs can be forgiven, and the offender is free from blame. On the other hand, shame is about our identity, about being bad, defective, wrong, irreparable, beyond redemption.

As a child, while my mother was a single parent—before the incredible man who would adopt me and forever be the one I called "Dad" came into the picture—I was a constant disappointment to my mother. I was undiagnosed at the time, struggling with ADHD, and my impulsivity kept me in constant trouble in school.

I got kicked out of kindergarten for writing a four-letter word on a girl's arm. Two kindergarten schools asked my mother not to bring me back. Finally, in first grade, the principal literally came down to the classroom and put me over his shoulder, with me kicking and screaming because I refused to leave the classroom when the teacher told me to go. I was terrified of being separated from the class, my shame already declaring me a defective kid.

In fourth grade, I had an African American male teacher who saw something good in me. He saw beyond my impulsivity and inability to control my behavior. He made me the line leader. He gave me tasks to do in the classroom. During recess, he sent an entire field of kids downfield in a game of touch football so that he could throw the ball to me, standing two feet away from him, ensuring that with a concerted, intentional, frightening effort on my part, I would catch the ball. He recognized that one of my other deficits was extreme incoordination—a product of an underdeveloped part of my brain—another result of being an extremely premature baby.

Standing with two hands on the ball, I beamed in the glow of his approval, and I felt something good about myself as I lingered at that moment. Later, when this same teacher hurt my feelings, I tried to kick him between the legs with all my might. He caught my foot—mission aborted. But he never turned away from me. Never was I as impacted by the affirmation and acceptance of another leader or authority figure as I was by him. God used a fourth-grade male teacher to show me what love looked like in the absence of a father's love.

Still, the layers of shame ran deep. My behavior, fueled by ADHD and the subsequent negative responses from the authority figures in my life, instilled in my young heart a sense of helplessness and hopelessness regarding my ability to do anything right, which made even the smallest victory or acknowledgment from an adult monumental in its impact.

However, my moments of triumph were too few and were vastly overshadowed by my "bad" behavior. Something big shifted inside of me in those early years that convinced me that I was just too wrong, too defective to be loved or the object of an adult's pleasure, and that my behavior would always betray me, leaving me naked and very much afraid of losing whatever love I could garner.

My mother was struggling and frustrated, and my perception of her anger and disappointment sealed a sense of inner "badness" in my soul in a way that fueled a self-fulfilling prophecy marked by continued impulsive and problematic behavior through my teenage years.

Years later, in my first year of college at Indiana University, I was sitting in church. The evangelist that was preaching became more animated as the anointing increased in the room. Mid-sentence, he stopped, whirled around, pointed his index finger at me, and said, "God has got His hand on you." His words were accompanied by a tangibly hot Presence of the Holy Spirit that burned like fire in my chest.

That was the first time I connected with my true destiny. It was the first time I felt very "right" and wanted, not like a total misfit. I knew at that moment that God loved me and that I had a promised future. That's a huge takeaway from a brief moment in a church service, but that small handful of powerful words from God to my heart was transformational. A few words uttered in the anointing of the Holy Spirit dismantled years of shaming messages that had been my constant food from the adults in my life who didn't know what to do with me. That was the beginning of my emergence from shame.

One word from God's heart can turn shame inside out. The only way we emerge from the hell of self and the voices in our heads that confirm our "not-enough-ness" is to look up and see Him and to hear Him speak to our hearts.

Pray this with me:

Jesus, I don't know where it all got started with me. All I know is that the bad stuff stuck, and I believed it. I look to You as the Creator of the Universe and as my Father and ask you to speak Your words of life to me. Father, two words from Your mouth to my ears are more powerful than a million pronouncements of failure made by imperfect humans who need the very thing I am asking from You. Speak to me now, in my dreams, and in moments when I least expect it. Tell me, Lord, who I am, and give me a glimpse into the pages of the Book of Life so that I can apprehend the promised future and destiny that You have created me for. I exist for You, Lord, and my purpose and true self are found in You alone. I stop right now and ask what You want to say to me. What is something You like about me? What is something You want me to know? (Now take a few minutes to listen). In Jesus' Name.

DAY 4

Naked and Unashamed

"Adam and his wife were both naked, and they felt no shame."

-NEW INTERNATIONAL VERSION, GEN. 2:25

A dam is symbolic of all humankind in his dissatisfaction with who he was and his longing to be more than he was. He suddenly felt a lack, a deficiency, that led him to partake of the fruit of the Tree of Knowledge of Good and Evil. In failing to accept his limitations, he lost his healthy shame (which alerts us to our boundaries), and yielded to his desire to be without constraints, making his shame toxic because of pride. Nakedness, in this narrative, is symbolic of the true and authentic self. In their nakedness, Adam and Eve were at home in their skin and had nothing to hide—naked, unashamed, vulnerable, honest. However, they opted to create false selves by refusing to accept their authentic selves and reaching to be more than their limitations would permit. Their shame transformed from the healthy shame that acknowledges limitation and boundaries into shame as a state of being that takes over one's entire identity.

Shame as an identity believes that one's being is hopelessly flawed and defective. This is called toxic shame. Toxic shame always demands a cover-up. So, one who abdicates the true self, opting for the illusory false self, ceases to exist psychologically.

In refusing to unconditionally love and accept our true selves — admittedly one of the most challenging tasks for all of humankind — we plummet into a lifetime of cover-up, secrecy, and hiding. Secrecy and the need to hide our true selves because of painful rejections is the fundamental root of all human suffering. Without self-love and acceptance, we are doomed to be held captive by a false self that we spend our life energy trying to maintain.[5]

One night, my wife, son, and I got into a conversation that sprung from a series we were watching on TV that had a plethora of family issues woven through the plot. We adopted our son, Rodney, just before his junior year in high school. He was a former student of mine and fulfilled a long-awaited promise from God to my wife and me of a son.

It is common for us to have conversations about his black family of origin and his history. His grandmother raised him and his three other siblings because his biological mother was in and out of prison. The family of origin for Rodney had a painful and rough history that included him being groomed to step into the family business as a drug lord. Before he reached his 10th birthday, he saw his oldest uncle shot and killed while he huddled in the floorboards of the back seat, hoping to escape notice.

His other uncles annihilated him with ritualistic abuse and terror tactics in their efforts to create a boy who was devoid of any emotion — an emotion that could betray him at any given moment. Tears were met with beatings, fortifying the bedrock of toxic shame that had become his heart. He was also familiar with poverty and deprivation.

---

[5] Bradshaw, J. (2015). Healing the shame that binds you. Health Communications.

Poverty, in and of itself, has its own brand of shame—it is worn and seen in the faces of those who have been generationally oppressed by it. Alcoholism was another mainstay in the environment. Alcoholism and poverty fit together frequently like a hand and glove. Alcohol provides a false sense of relief at a moment in time while furthering the work of poverty and destroying any hope of emergence. The fact that Rodney studied at a Christian college on a football scholarship, fell in love, and married a beautiful and amazing woman, is a testimony of God's extreme grace. This account is but a brief snapshot of the nightmare that was our son's life for many years.

Rodney, like his younger siblings, was excited for Christmas morning. The same uncle that Rodney would witness getting shot a couple of years later had orchestrated a cruel training exercise. The kids were all up, and gifts were distributed in haste, and he was caught up in the reverie of seeing his brother and sisters' delight with a gift that had been hoped for but not guaranteed, making this moment even sweeter. He waited, thinking that Grandma had given the younger siblings first dibs on unwrapping their gifts, and now his turn had come. But... nothing.

In a surreal split second, like a slow-motion scene in a movie, he looked around, taking in the whole picture, seeing his siblings, and realized that he had been left out. His stomach sank like a lead cannonball in an ocean.

Later, he looked under the Christmas tree again, wondering if maybe he had missed something, when Uncle Bebe said, "What are you looking under there for? There ain't nothin' for you." As Rodney delivered the punchline in the retelling of this story, I felt like I had been sucker-punched, and my mouth hung open as I processed what he just said. Finally,

I blurted, "So, you didn't get anything?!" Even in the retelling of the story, a fresh wave of shame flooded his countenance.

I felt my neck flush when hearing and seeing my son relive an excruciatingly disheartening memory of an event that took place when he was seven years old. How do you shift gears in the middle of that awkward moment when a conversation about a shaming incident regenerates a familiar pang in your stomach? The only shift that works to change the atmosphere of shame is for the Truth to show up.

Jesus said in John 10:10, "A thief has only one thing in mind—he wants to steal, slaughter, and destroy. But I have come to give you everything in abundance, more than you expect—life in its fullness until you overflow!" (The Passion Translation). He also said, "...if you embrace the truth, it will release true freedom into your lives" (TPT, John 8:32). So, I spoke truth over my son. "You are loved and you are enough."

We cannot change what has happened in our lives that produced shame, making us feel defective and wrong. Truth is a Person, and His Name is Jesus. Jesus stands outside of time. Knowing that Jesus was present with us in the most devastating moments enables us to find resolve. Our unhealed perception of God's absence is what He wants to reveal and heal. I heard Bill Johnson (Senior Pastor at Bethel Church in Redding, California) say once [my paraphrase] that "the biggest problem in Christendom is the belief that God is not Good."

Perception is everything. Often, when looking back at some of our most painful memories, others' intentions are not what needs to be healed. It's our perception of what happened that Jesus must come into, revealing His Presence with us. He has never abandoned us—ever! The enemy knows our perceptual vulnerabilities and has an investment in the lie that we were alone, abandoned, rejected, unloved. TRUTH breaks the power of the lie.

I want to invite you into an encounter with Jesus, even now. Instead of repeating a prayer or making a declaration, I am asking Jesus to encounter you, in this moment now (or whenever you can set aside a little time. Set a timer for 15 minutes if you're pressed for time. But don't skip over this step). Christians can get weirded out when we use the word "visualize" or "meditate," but the New Agers did not invent the words or the practice. God gave you your imagination — the screen of your heart — for a very good reason.

Here's the exercise:

Get still before the Lord and ask the Holy Spirit to show you a time when you felt intense shame. After an instance or event comes to mind, ask Jesus where He was in the picture. As you take this step, Jesus is going to reveal Himself somewhere in the picture. You may see Him merely being present. You may see Him intervening in some way or speaking something to you. The key is to allow yourself to visualize the scenario and let the Holy Spirit fill the picture for you without limiting how He will show up.

For some, it may just be a simple assurance and knowing in your heart that Jesus was present with you and His Presence covers you in the place you feel exposed. For others, Jesus will appear as you imagine and visualize the scene. Still others may hear him speak a word of comfort, assurance, or affirmation.

Encountering you is something Jesus longs to do. He longs to reveal Himself to you in a way that your mind and, more importantly, your heart can apprehend. Blessings to you as you venture into a place of encountering Jesus. Feel free to do this exercise as often as you want. There are no limits here. Make sure you write down what you see and hear so you can go back and remember. One experience builds on the other as He heals your heart from pain and trauma and reveals His heart for you. Feel free to take a prayer partner or spouse if you feel like you need help. He will meet you where you are.

DAY 5

Shame, Contempt and Violence

'But when she took it to him to eat, he grabbed her and said, "Come to bed with me, my sister." "No, my brother!" she said to him. "Don't force me! Such a thing should not be done in Israel! Don't do this wicked thing...Then Amnon hated her with intense hatred. In fact, he hated her more than he had loved her. Amnon said to her, "Get up and get out!" "No!" she said to him. "Sending me away would be a greater wrong than what you have already done to me."'

-*NIV*, 2 SAM. 13:11-12 & 15-16

Shame is not just a consequence of the Fall of Man, it is an emotional weapon in the enemy's hand to corrupt and destroy our relationships with God and each other. Shame in the enemy's hand disrupts our giftedness, disintegrates our God-given talents and creativity, and hampers any endeavor that promotes goodness, beauty, and joy in the lives of others, shutting us down as light-bearers to the world.[6]

The problem with shame, and the reason we need to allow the Holy Spirit to heal us, is that shame is not just a feeling, it is the all-pervasive dictator of our souls and a product of sin — our own and that which has been committed against us.

---

[6] Thompson, C. (2015). The soul of shame: Retelling the stories we believe about ourselves. Downers Grove, IL: InterVarsity Press.

All evil is directly connected to shame. However, one does not need to be evil to experience the impact of shame—one simply needs to be human in a fallen world. The debilitating effect of shame on our souls can be seen on a continuum. The further we move along the continuum, the more toxic and dangerous the influence of shame becomes.

The internalization of shame can either be very subtle or quite overt. Because it permeates the very soil of our hearts, rendering them less fertile in their capacity to produce the fruits of the Spirit, all shame in the soil is a contaminant—a contaminant that Jesus bore on His body. Therefore, we can be free of it. Just because you may not be able to visualize what freedom looks like—freedom from specific patterns, struggles, addictions, and destructive mindsets you are all too familiar with—does not mean you cannot be free.

In the story of Amnon and Tamar, Amnon, David's firstborn son, driven by lust, pursues his virgin half-sister, luring her deceitfully as he feigned illness in his premeditated plan to rape her. We do not know precisely what kind of father David was, but we know that he was a man after God's own heart despite his moral failures. However, he was not exempt from the consequences he would reap because of his failures. He reaped them not only in his kingdom but more personally, in his family—a snapshot of what generational sin looks like.

What makes Amnon's story particularly heinous is Tamar's desperate plea, begging, "No, my brother!" she said to him. "Don't force me! Such a thing should not be done in Israel! Don't do this wicked thing. What about me? Where could I get rid of my disgrace? And what about you? You would be like one of the wicked fools in Israel. Please speak to the king; he will not keep me from being married to you." But he refused to listen to her, and since he was stronger than she, he raped her

(*NIV*, 2 Sam. 13: 12-14).

Tamar appealed to her brother to make the situation right (as much as it could be under a patriarchal system) through marriage, but violence, not marriage, was what Satan baited the hook with. Tragically for all involved, Amnon eagerly took it hook, line, and sinker. Demonic influence is often the precursor to violent and denigrating behavior. Shame can be diabolical in its demand and compulsion for compliance with evil. But we cannot opt out of taking responsibility for our behavior because "the devil made me do it." The demonic has no place or authority over us except by permission, whether that be explicit or implicit in our failure to say no to the behavior at hand.

John Wimber[7], the leader of the Vineyard church planting movement in the '80s, had a simple analogy about demonic influence and Christians. We cannot be "possessed" by the devil; however, as he often said regarding the demonic, "there ain't no flies where there's no garbage." Wimber contended that demons could only have a powerful influence in the places where we have already given permission through our behavior or through things we have inadvertently come into agreement with.

Toxic shame becomes the core of neurosis, character disorders, political violence, wars, and criminality, coming the closest in defining what human bondage looks like.[8] Shame is

---

[7] John Wimber, leader of the Vineyard movement in his lifetime, impacted the lives of thousands across the globe – and was used by God to renew the spiritual life of the 20th and 21st century Church (John Wimber, n.d.)." Retrieved from https://vineyardusa.org/about/john-wimber/

[8] Bradshaw, J. (2015). Healing the shame that binds you. Health Communications.

not experienced in a vacuum and is not benign—it must have a target. It moves in two directions—inward toward the self or outward to another. It either gets turned inward in debilitating self-contempt or is turned outward in blame, disparagement (verbal abuse), other-centered contempt, humiliation, and violence, which is evidenced in the rest of the narrative of the rape of Tamar.

Our story tells us that after Amnon forcibly raped his sister, he "... hated her with intense hatred. In fact, he hated her more than he had loved her. Amnon said to her, "Get up and get out!" "No!" she said to him. "Sending me away would be a greater wrong than what you have already done to me" (*NIV*, 2 Sam. 13:15-16).

Many of us have been on one or both ends of shame—we have been the target of shame, contempt, and violence, or we have been the perpetrator. The answer for both the perpetrator and the victim is the same—Jesus. In our closing prayer in today's devotional, I would like to go in both directions. As the saying goes—hurt(ing) people hurt people. Judgment has already fallen on the Crucified One; therefore, we are free regardless of which side of shame we're on.

As ones who have marinated in self-contempt because of the places where we have had the shame of another foisted upon us, it is time to let ourselves off the hook. The three most prominent barriers to personal wholeness are the failure to forgive others, failure to forgive ourselves, and inability to accept ourselves.[9] Once we are able to overcome these three things, we discover freedom from shame and are able to become fully present and integrated into our relationship to God, others, and ourselves.

---

[9] Payne, L. (1984). The broken image: Restoring personal wholeness through healing prayer. Wheaton, IL: Crossway Books.

Many times, we must articulate and declare a truth before our heart apprehends it. Life and death are in the power of the tongue (*NIV*, Prov. 8:21), so we must declare what is truth and life to ourselves and regarding others. We must move in the opposite spirit of that which is afflicting us to employ the workings of Heaven and the Kingdom of God on our behalf. All things flow through honor in the Kingdom of God. It is not hypocritical to declare a truth that my heart has yet to fully integrate. In the framing up of the reality, we articulate in the spirit, out of our mouths, that we will see the fruit manifest. We start by blessing our story, our history in all its ugliness, bumps, and blemishes. Next, we bless those who persecuted us because they failed to apprehend who they were created to be in Christ.

Pray this with me:

Lord, I bless my story. You know all that is in it—the parts I am unaware of, the parts I have acknowledged to myself, but not to another, and those I have yet to own. You know my beginning from the end. You knew me before my earthly parents conceived me. I bless every part of my story — everything I have done that I regret and all that was done to me by others. I do not bless the evil, but I bless everything that has been part of making me into the person I am today and the one you continue to make me into. All darkness is light to You. I thank You that nothing is too dark for Your Love and Redemption to lighten.

I also bless those that have been the target of my shame and anger, I receive Your forgiveness, and I release myself from further torment and shame in my failure to forgive and accept myself. I choose to let myself off the hook in Jesus' Name. I cannot crucify myself to satisfy my own self-contempt. I receive what You already did as the Crucified and Resurrected One for me, delivering me from the "hell" of myself.

I repent for every attempt I have made to satisfy my need for justice. You alone, Lord Jesus, have the power to pardon me and those who have hurt me. You pardon both the victim and the perpetrator. I thank You for Your Grace and Freedom in my heart and life. In Jesus' Name. Amen.

DAY 6

Two Prostitutes

Vivian: "People put you down enough—you start to believe it."
Edward: "I think you are a very bright, very special woman."
Vivian: "The bad stuff is easier to believe. You ever notice that?"

-EXCERPT FROM PRETTY WOMAN[10]

For those of you who aren't familiar with it, Pretty Woman was a 1990's film starring Julia Roberts and Richard Gere that made everyone fall in love with a prostitute. We fell in love with the modern-day Cinderella story for the same reason we find ourselves championing Cinderella in the Disney cartoon. Making the Cinderella character a prostitute certainly brought more grit and sex to the story, but the essential elements are still the same. We love Cinderella because we relate to her identity crisis as one who has been despised, hated, and envied for their true identity and potential. Like Cinderella, we have been sold a bill of lies about who we are—making our perception of ourselves the most formidable obstacle for us to overcome to embrace our promised future.

In a revealing scene, Edward Lewis asks Vivian why she

[10] Marshall, G. (Director). (1990, March 23). Pretty Woman [Video file]. Retrieved from https://www.imdb.com/title/tt0100405/

became a prostitute, and without all the details that led her into her current vocation, she simply says, "The bad stuff is easier to believe. You ever notice that?"

In another scene, Vivian recounts her mother telling her that if there were 51 men in a room, and 50 of them were good, and one was a bum, she would be drawn to the one. Vivian claims that she is a "bum magnet." Essentially, Vivian is saying that the labels stuck. The bad things that were spoken over her had overpowered the good—they were the only words that mattered. "Death and life are in the power of the tongue..." (*The New King James Version*, Prov. 18:21).

When I talk about identity to my Bible Literature students from the book of Genesis, I talk about Pretty Woman. Her story is a good example of how words have leverage in shaping our perceptions of who we are. I present them with a hypothetical situation and ask this question, "If I constantly told my daughter as she was growing up that she was ugly and stupid, when in reality she was uber-smart and beautiful, what do you think she would believe?" They always affirm that she would believe that she was ugly and stupid—words matter. Words become shapers of our identity, and negative words fortify the foundation of shame in our hearts.

Jesus encountered a prostitute as a guest in Simon the Pharisee's house (Luke 7:36-50). Simon questioned Jesus' prophetic abilities when a known prostitute came with an alabaster jar of perfume, anointing His feet with the perfume and her tears while wiping them with her hair.

Jesus, in His love for both the Pharisee and the sinner, did not go off on Simon but did what He did the best in speaking to this generation—He told a story. He told a story about two debtors, both forgiven the debt, but one of them owed ten times the amount of the other. Jesus asked Simon which of the debtors would love the moneylender more. He answered correctly and said, "I suppose the one who had the bigger debt forgiven" (*NIV*, Luke 7:43).

What Jesus did next should have turned Simon on his head if he realized the economy of what Jesus was doing. Jesus always had a way of confronting multiple issues simultaneously without looking like that was his primary agenda. Jesus "turned toward the woman and said to Simon, 'Do you see this woman?'" (*NIV*, Luke 7:44). He did not say, "do you see this prostitute?" He said, "woman." In calling her a woman, Jesus was restoring her identity while simultaneously healing her shame in an open forum. Jesus did not respond to this woman in a way that affirmed her deep shame and humiliation—He affirmed her "true self," not the "false self" she had become familiar with in her sinful behavior and in the responses from those who abused and degraded her.

After His public restoration of this woman's identity and peeling back the veil of shame in which she had been enshrouded for many years, He contrasted Simon's lack of attentiveness as a host with her extravagant worship, remorse, and gratitude. She had just been cleansed and delivered from all the indignity of her past. Jesus said, "I tell you, her many sins have been forgiven—as her great love has shown. But whoever has been forgiven little loves little" (*NIV*, Luke 7:47).

Without calling Simon out in a way that would have shamed him, Jesus did give Simon much to think about. He highlighted the judgment in his heart, his lack of revelation of who Jesus was, which would have warranted a worshipful response, the disconnect in his perception of sin, and his faulty premise that "getting it right" is what God is after. "Getting it right" is a religious construct that seeks to gain Heaven's approval through works. Being in right standing with God has to do with authenticity of the heart—coming to Jesus as ones who are broken, have failed many times to "get it right" in our own power, and who realize that One "got it right" for all. It is His sacrifice alone that makes us right. As Jesus says to this woman at the end of the narrative, "Your faith has saved you; go in peace (*NIV*, Luke 7:50)."

Pray this with me:

Lord, deliver me from my inner Pharisee whose voice solely serves to keep me trapped in shame and the sense of being irreparably flawed—beyond the grasp of Your Grace. Help me recognize and quickly label the voice of the Pharisee as my accuser and shut it down quickly with my words. Deliver me from the temptation to agree with my accuser when my past mistakes threaten to haunt me. I say no to that voice. Father, I submit the canvas of my life to you and invite you to paint a new picture—paint me into my destiny and promised future.

Open the book of my life and give me a glimpse of the chapters that lie ahead. Heal my perception of the bad stuff in my story—reducing what feels like volumes in the saga of my life to a mere sentence. I look to you as the Creator to tell me who I really am—to affirm my true self, not the false one that emerged from the rubble of my past. As an act of faith, I choose to embrace the right standing and righteousness that You give me. I am right because You are Right. I will declare the truth of who I am with my mouth until my heart apprehends it. In Jesus' Name. Amen.

DAY 7

A Room Divided

When they kept on questioning him, he straightened up and said to them, "Let any one of you who is without sin be the first to throw a stone at her."

-NIV, JOHN 8:7

I have taught Bible Literature in a public school in the South for 12 years. I was the first in our district to teach it. When my department head sent an email asking who would be interested in teaching this class, I shot off my reply without thinking or hesitating. "I will." I had no idea what I was signing up for or why, but I sensed there was Someone orchestrating a set-up. Every class has its dynamics, and no two classes have been the same. I have students regularly journal and respond to relevant topics that are important to them and then I use their questions about how the Bible or God relates to the issues on the top of their list to ignite discussion.

One way to sidestep the issue of giving a potentially "faith-based" response in the context of a "literature" class is the use of metaphor. Everything in the Bible is a metaphor; it also happens to be true! For example, being created in God's image is both a tangible faith reality and a multifaceted metaphoric concept with far-reaching implications.

During one semester, I had a class that totally baffled me. I have always been okay with having a broad mix of students in my class. I know that the class is a favorite among students professing to be Christians. I also know that sometimes students get plopped into a class because it's the only class that works with their schedule, while others are seekers and are curiously drawn to take the class. In this class, I had a professing atheist who I loved because she asked questions that most would shy away from. She was honest, authentic, and raw. I was ecstatic.

But something strange happened when I attempted to engage the class in a conversation over topics and questions they submitted in their journals. Silence can be painful and awkward in a classroom, and the potential for opposing views requires a facilitator who can employ both honor and grace to all sides and who is not afraid of things getting messy. In the bits of conversation that by an act of God took place in my attempt at group discussion, I realized that the room was divided into two—literally. Those professing Christ all sat on one side of the room, and the seekers and my resident atheist sat on the opposite side of the room. In addition, the layout of desks in the room divided the room with rows of students facing each other. So, not only was this dichotomy very apparent by where students sat but the room itself was split.

After several attempts to get a class discussion going, I threw in the towel and wrote off any hope I had of engaging them. Finally, I asked the question, "Ok, someone tell me why it's so challenging to talk in this class?" My atheist kicked things off and proceeded to tell me that she tried talking to four of the girls from the other side of the room outside of class to get to know them. As she recounted the next part, the hurt, betrayal, anger, and shame was apparent on her face.

She said that each person she met with did all the talking and never once asked her what she thought—about God or anything else—and to make matters worse, they tried to convert her. She felt preached at. In her eyes, she wasn't a person but a project, or a prize to be won. It wasn't the intentions of the other girls (which may have been more innocent) that impacted her, it was her perception of how they reacted to her. Shame, as we have discussed earlier, goes in two directions. It either turns inward in self-contempt or is projected onto another as a target. In projecting our shame onto others, we elevate ourselves in a feeble and illegitimate attempt to keep it from landing on our own heads and suffocating us.

Assuming the girl's account of the story was accurate, it's a fair question to ask what shame the "Christian" students had that they foisted upon the professing atheist. Answer? I can't be sure because I can't attribute motive in this scenario. However, historically Christians are guilty of seeing evangelism as a duty to be fulfilled in their own attempt to "get it right." My sense is that my atheist student felt the weight of what felt like religious duty and what they were told in church that they "should" do.

One doesn't usually feel exploited in a vacuum. Some forms of shame are internal and do not require an agent to function as the "shamer." My atheist student felt exploited because she felt the agenda to "win" her rather than simply know her. I felt a wave of shame come over me as I felt embarrassed at what happened and was saddened over this quagmire in the room that I now needed to navigate. My human response was to feel shame as a Christian and slightly humiliated as a teacher because of the responsibility I felt for preserving everyone. I could've let shame take over and blamed myself, but the truth is that I could not control what went on outside of the class. At this moment, I could build a bridge, or it could all crash and burn, ending badly.

I apologized to my atheist student and asked her for

forgiveness as a Believer. I couldn't call the Christian girls out publicly because I didn't want to place shame on them either. The truth is that we were all learning, and this was a teachable moment. Though I'm sure they had not intended it, they had hurt this young lady. What I could do is repent for them by proxy and model what I knew was right. As I asked my atheist to forgive me as a Christian for what she experienced as dishonoring, something broke in the room, and there was a tangible Grace to forgive. I was also able to address the rift between to two sides of the room while even acknowledging that their struggles were identical, which I realized after a few minutes of honest sharing from both sides of the room.

Ironically, both sides of the room felt judged by the other. The Christians felt judged by the seekers and unbelievers because they thought they had to be perfect because they were "Christians." The other side of the room felt judged by the Christians because they felt they were under scrutiny for their freely acknowledged behaviors. In that way, the unbelieving side of the room was more authentic because they didn't hide their shameful behavior—the fact that they struggled with sex, drugs, and self-destructive habits employed to lessen the stress they felt in their lives. The Christians felt the need to project a perfect image, and it's something the world can see right through. Truth and honesty break the walls down.

I gave my observation that both sides of the room were terrified of being judged by the other, and everyone in the room was struggling with the same temptations and cultural pressures. I told them that they could be safe in sharing honestly through honoring one another. We declared it a judgment-free zone. I would love to say that after this breakthrough and mutual acceptance of each other, we spent the rest of the semester in communication bliss. We didn't. But

we all learned a lot about the power of judgment. And I became more acutely aware of the kind of shame that religion brings with it.

In Jesus' day, the Pharisees were pompous, proud, and self-righteous, but they were also steeped in scandal and corruption because they sought to satisfy the need to be "good enough" through getting it right and keeping the law. At least on the outside. They tried to get it right down to the last jot and tittle of the law, but ironically, they broke their own rules frequently to serve their selfish purposes.

God is always after the heart first, not outward behavior, because what's in the heart drives behavior. My prayer is that my students learned something valuable, that relationship always trumps "getting it right" and mercy always triumphs over judgment. I hope they apprehended the truth that both sides of the room can't ever get it right through good behavior. Only One got it right, and He made a way for both sides of the room—those on the left who thought they had already gotten it right and those on the right who were profoundly aware that they had not. Jesus died for both, and both are redeemed and lose their shame at the foot of the Crucified One.

Pray this with me:

Lord, I am laying down all my religion in exchange for a relationship. I choose to know You over trying to clean up and get it right to earn something You have freely given me. Show me how to "be" rather than "do." Deliver me, Lord, from the tyranny of "getting it right" and my feeble attempts to manage my life. I want transformation, Lord, and You are the Great Transformer. Connect my head to my heart and free me from striving to please You. I call my spirit to the forefront, to lead my soul (including my heart and my head) and body and to align with You. My heart is Yours, Lord, so come and do in it what I cannot. In Jesus' Name. Amen.

DAY 8

Silencing the Voice of the Enemy

"...If you know the enemy and know yourself, you need not fear the result of a hundred battles. If you know yourself but not the enemy, for every victory gained, you will also suffer defeat...If you know neither the enemy nor yourself, you will succumb in every battle."

-THE ART OF WAR, SUN TZU[11]

O ne of the most beguiling and devious deceptions that the devil has ever bestrewn in Christendom at large is the substitution of the worship of God in spirit and truth for the worship of the rational mind—particularly in Western Christianity. In our endeavor to always be reasonable and sensible, we have embraced a very cerebral Christianity that relegates the supernatural to the absurd and illogical. There is nothing wrong with having a brain, being an educated person, and seeking wisdom in all things. But, when we relegate everything to reason and rely on our abilities to solve every problem and challenge on earth, we deny and nullify the voice of God in our midst.

We also attribute the enemy's accusations, lies, and distortions to our own voice. The result is that we don't hear

---

[11] Tzu, S. (2010). The art of war [PDF]. Capstone Publishing.

what God is saying, and we normalize the enemy's voice in our heads. Often our only weapon of warfare is to get busy to distract ourselves, or to do something else to numb or drown out the voices. In doing so, we lose on every front.

Add in "religion," and we relationally and socially excommunicate anyone who claims to hear the voice of God and make the assertion that the gifts of the Holy Spirit are relevant for today. Religion makes fun of the devil, trivializing the full-front assault that he wages against our minds, hearts, and emotions. Religion trades off hearing God's voice for a five-year business plan for church growth and a plethora of new programs and fundraising campaigns. Religion shames the spiritual, calling it creepy, extremist, unstable, ungodly, overly emotional, immature, and an assault against good reason.

Reasonable people don't pray in the spirit or call forth a generation into their prophetic destinies and promised futures. Reasonable people don't go with what's in their hearts to move toward God, actively listen for His Voice, or engage in ministry. Instead, responsible Christians feel bad about their sins they committed that week and go to the altar so they can religiously repent and work on "getting it right" the next week. Rinse and repeat.

Here's the deal. Jesus said, "My sheep hear my voice, and I know them, and they follow me" (*English Standard Version*, John 10:27). John 17 spells out our union with Christ. He prays for all the ones who would be coming into union with the Father, that they all may be one; just as You, Father, are in Me and I in You, "that they also may be one in Us, so that the world may believe [without any doubt] that You sent Me" (*Amplified Bible*, John 17:21).

John also said, "And we know that the Son of God has come and has given us understanding, so that we may know him who is true; and we are in him who is true, in His Son Jesus Christ. He is the true God and eternal life" (*ESV*, 1 John 5:20). We have the fullness of the Godhead dwelling inside us, in our spirits, and we are one with Him. This one truth, when truly understood, can dismantle years of shame!

One of my English teacher friends was doing some fun stuff with photos that blended someone's picture with a juxtaposed reflection of another character, and when I saw them, I had to have one for my school ID. She asked me who I wanted to be juxtaposed with, and I said, "Well, Jesus, of course!" So, she put it together for me.

When I was showing off my new ID, one teacher who wasn't a believer said he thought it looked sacrilegious. I told him it was not, because it was a picture of my union with Christ. When I look to see the reflection of myself in the water, I see Jesus. It encapsulated a concept that I enjoy explaining to everyone who sees it on my ID or as my screen saver on my computer.

Here's the rest of the deal. I recently made a new policy regarding hearing God's voice and how I would respond to it. My new policy is that everything in me (desires, promptings, thoughts to bless, inclinations in the moment, passions, ideas, and more) is likely coming from Jesus, as long as it doesn't violate the Word of God and is life-giving. I don't have to ask a million questions of God, "Is this You or me?" If what is in me promotes the Kingdom, blesses, or loves people, then I will assume it is Jesus, and I am not giving it a second thought. I believe that God is speaking to me and through me as me. He wants me to re-present Himself to the world, not as someone other than me, but through me, like me—a unique expression of Jesus in the world that only I can do. What is the worst-case scenario? That I accidentally love or bless someone? Even at that, it would be God's heart to do so.

Because we have so rationalized the enemy's voice as just our bad thoughts, we need to use our words to take captive everything thought that goes through our head. If the thoughts, even the ones that I think are "just me," are accusing, lying, derogatory, demeaning, or self-deprecating, they are from the devil—period. Jesus never talks to us in that manner.

My new policy on hearing God's voice, as both words I hear Him speak to me and the impressions, inclinations, and musings of my heart and mind, is that I am not overly questioning them as long as they are in agreement with His Word. I am acting on them knowing that my Daddy is good and that anything that blesses, promotes, encourages, or impacts the Kingdom of Heaven is birthed out the union that I have with Him. Loving and following Jesus has always been simple—easy. If it feels complicated, you are probably doing religion or some other dysfunction—not a relationship.

Pray this with me:

Jesus, I thank You that You are ONE with me. I am in YOU, and YOU are in ME. I have a new policy when it comes to trying to discern Your voice and Your will for me. I choose to have faith in the union that I have with You and trust that the desires and inclinations of my heart to bless, love, and do things that advance Your Kingdom on earth are Heavenly in their origin. I use my voice to come out of agreement with any and every thought that comes into my head (even the ones that I have become familiar with as my self-talk) that accuses, lies to me, or tears me down. They are straight from the pit of hell, and I will NOT entertain them. I ask for the grace to break out of my familiar patterns of accepting the enemy's darts as my self-defeating mantras. I am going to do "simple", Lord, because You are simple. I am choosing to trust more in Your ability to keep me than the devil's ability to pull me away from You. Thank You, Father, that You have made a way through Your Son for me to have continuous, unbroken fellowship with You. In Jesus Name. Amen.

DAY 9

You Are Not Your DNA

"Therefore if any person is [ingrafted] in Christ (the Messiah), he is a new creation (a new creature altogether); the old [previous moral and spiritual condition] has passed away. Behold, the fresh and new has come!"

-AMPLIFIED BIBLE, CLASSIC EDITION, 2 COR. 5:17

Dr. Dan Allender[12], a pioneer in a unique approach to trauma and abuse therapy, says that the quest to know and understand our story finds its origin in our desire to know who we are and why it matters that we are who we are. Allender says, "It is not I who must be found. Instead, it is God who is to be found. He waits—quietly, passionately, and winsomely—within my story. All I must do is ask, seek, and knock." He asserts that we need to know who shares the stage with us, which is sometimes apparent as we look at our parents, siblings, spouse, grandparents, friends, mentors, and even abusers. Sometimes, according to Allender, the people we barely know, those who stand in the shadows off-stage, carry secrets to our story. The people who have shared our life stage have had a hand in defining us, telling us who we are.

I like telling a story to my students with an obvious

---

[12] Allender, D. B., & Fann, L. K. (2005). To be told. know your story, shape your future. Colorado Springs, CO: WaterBrook Press.

conclusion that makes them stop and think. I paint a picture of two brothers growing up in similar family backgrounds like alcoholism. Both are abused, watch abuse in the family, and are traumatized. One becomes just like his alcoholic abuser, perpetuating the generational cycle. The other becomes a successful parent and has success in his life endeavors.

The question is, "What is the difference between these two people who had similar backgrounds with different outcomes in their lives?" Within a short amount of time in the discussion, they land on "choices" as the single most significant difference in the outcomes. I always elaborate on how the one who breaks the cycle chooses not to be a victim of their circumstances or allow what happened to define who he is. It is not what happens to us, but rather how we respond to what happens, that determines who we become.

There is an old bumper sticker that says, "S*&t Happens." That is true. We all live in a fallen world and things happen to us that we cannot control. The impact that it has on our heart, soul, and psyche may look different. But when we peel away the circumstances and the specific happenings of our lives that were painful, we find our places of commonality with those we're journeying with. Our human propensity to self-protect becomes the seedbed for our later dysfunctional ways of dealing with the pangs of death that have invaded our soul.

What we experience as "death" (e.g., rejection, abandonment, deprivation) we unconsciously make a vow never to experience in the same way again. That vow threads the needle of the defenses woven into the tapestry of our lives, creating patterns of relating that are designed to avoid pain. For example, when a young girl experiences a violent crime like rape, she may vow never to allow a man to hurt her again. Vows do not necessarily function with great specificity, but instead, they can be blanket statements that are much more pervasive in their reach, causing us to be alienated from a part of ourselves that we will be challenged to integrate later in life if we want to heal and grow.

My high school girlfriend was raised in a family where her father devalued her mother. In her perception, her mother was weak, a victim, and lacked the courage to stand up for herself while her misogynistic husband ran rough-shod over her. On the other hand, her father was strong and powerful in his brokenness and inability to consider, yield to, or engage with his wife. She made a vow that if her mother was the epitome of what it meant to be a woman, she didn't want to be one. Her vow cut her off from significant aspects of her gender. She later engaged in a lesbian relationship in her attempt to integrate with parts of herself that she felt estranged and cut off from.

An illustration that I like to use about brokenness is, if you took ten drinking glasses and dropped them all from the same height, they all break differently. In the generation that comes through my classroom doors, I see many configurations of broken glasses. The circumstances under which the glasses break varies greatly, but the core areas of need and wounding are the same. We must abandon the assumption that we are the sum total of the way our glass breaks as predetermined by our DNA.

As new creations in Christ, we have a Heavenly DNA that supersedes and overrides our physical DNA. The DNA of our birth does not bind us because our citizenship is in Heaven. There is no such thing in Heaven's economy as "once this way, always this way." Brain science today validates that our thoughts can literally change our DNA. In the Kingdom of God, all limits are gone. The blood of Jesus is not limited in its ability to produce change. The blood of Jesus takes us beyond all that we could think or imagine in our union with Christ.

There are no limits other than that which we place on ourselves by the way we think and what we believe in our hearts. The reality is that as Believers, we have already been fashioned into the image of the One who made us. Just because we cannot imagine what freedom or radical transformation in our bodies, minds, and hearts look like does not mean that it does not exist. Sometimes, we must have an encounter with Heaven to open us up to further encounters.

Here's a simple truth: The Unseen Real is more real than the seen. When you frame up your world with Truth based on the Word of God, declare it with your mouth and engage it with your imagination, you can step into that which your words have created and see it become your new reality. Our words, inspired by Heavenly revelation, do not fall to the ground when we declare and speak them out. Instead, they connect with the Holy Spirit, the God of the Universe, to frame and build tangible realities on earth in our own lives and in the lives of those we carry in our hearts.

Pray this with me:

Father, I declare that I am not limited to my earthly DNA. I receive all the good that You have for me from every generation that preceded me. I ask that every mantle, anointing, gifting, and blessing that got dropped, thwarted, wasted, or missed in the previous generations would come to me. I ask that Your Heavenly DNA would override my earthly DNA and that You would fashion me into the man or woman of Your dreams, Lord. I declare that my Heavenly DNA trumps my earthly DNA. I thank You that I am becoming all You created me to be. I renounce every curse in my generational family of origin, every destructive pattern, every kind of sickness and disease, and every propensity for ungodliness in the strong, powerful, Name of Jesus! I thank You, Lord, that NONE of that comes to me or my children, and I am free from the curse of the law. Thank you, LORD. Amen.

DAY 10

You Manifest What You Believe

"How much more will the blood of Christ, who through the eternal [Holy] Spirit willingly offered Himself unblemished [that is, without moral or spiritual imperfection as a sacrifice] to God, cleanse your conscience from dead works and lifeless observances to serve the ever-living God?"

-AMPC, Heb. 9:14

Christians often get confused about what it means to be forgiven and cleansed from all sin and sin-consciousness by the blood of Jesus. The enemy has always been invested in the church, perpetuating the lie most have been taught, that we are just "sinners saved by grace." Many never move beyond their consciousness of how depraved they are as fallen humans.

Institutionalized religion loves this because a church full of believers whose primary goal is to manage their lives and get it right so they can be "good Christians" will thrive on a diet of shame that reinforces their primary belief about themselves. They will forever be caught on the hamster wheel of performing righteous-looking acts to redeem an unredeemable condition through striving. They will work themselves into oblivion, outwardly living up to the expectations of a fleshly, cultural Christianity that is devoid of power and impotent to transform those imprisoned in the "hell of self." This prison of navel-gazing introspection annihilates any opportunity for experiencing true peace. This peace can only come through the eradication of sin-consciousness through faith in the righteousness of the Crucified One. The Crucified and Resurrected One paid the price for us to not only be free from sin itself but from our hyper-consciousness of sin, guilt and shame.

What does this mean? What am I saying? Am I saying that we do not sin or will never sin? No. I am saying that only faith in the Righteousness of the One who paid the price for ALL to experience freedom from the burden of sin can truly deliver us from the futility of always trying to get it right and living in the endless cycle of "sin, shame, sin, repeat."

Therefore, there is now no condemnation [no guilty verdict, no punishment] for those who are in Christ Jesus [who believe in Him as personal Lord and Savior]. For the law of the Spirit of life [which is] in Christ Jesus [the law of our new being] has set you free from the law of sin and of death (*AMP*, Rom. 8:1-2).

We have so rationalized the voice of the enemy, whose primary job is to keep us locked tight in a place of accusation and condemnation, that we relegate our self-destructive thinking to just being "up in our heads" too much. The reality is that every thought that wreaks condemnation and accusation is straight from the pit of Hell and needs to be told to "shut up" in Jesus' Name! That bedrock of shame in our hearts that has been built on the foundation of rejection, abandonment, and abuse, along with the shaming responses of others, is too easily receptive to the darts of the enemy because our heart agrees with the voices that affirm our perception of depravity and self-contempt. The only way to break the agreement of our shame and a constant barrage of death that the enemy sows in the soil of our hearts is to take every thought captive.

We must be intentional about what we allow to dominate our headspace and not give shame and the enemy a playdate in our heads. The product of a life lived addicted to "getting it right," as opposed to believing by faith in the finished work of the Cross and its power to usher me into the righteousness of Jesus, is that we will continue to manifest sin while being tormented by our broken perception of who we are in relationship to God. Consequently, we fail to lay hold of our destiny, promised future, and calling in Christ. This is the enemy's ultimate goal—to sideline you, rendering you impotent in the Kingdom of God. We are destroying sophisticated arguments and every exalted and proud thing that sets itself up against the [true] knowledge of God, and we are taking every thought and purpose captive to the obedience of Christ..." (*AMP*, 2 Cor. 10:5).

Bill Johnson[13] has aptly stated it this way: "I can't afford to have a thought about me in my head that He doesn't have in His head about me. Any time it entertains things that are not absolutely true and central in His perspective about me, then I'm visiting something that will war against what He thinks about me." If we want to manifest righteousness, we must be intentional about what we will and won't listen to and what comes out of our mouths. One of the greatest tools of Heaven to transform a heart of shame is the Word of God and the declarations that issue forth from His word to frame up a new reality for us to walk in—the reality of being righteous because He is righteous.

---

[13] Bill Johnson | Quotes. (2014, September 20). Retrieved from https://melwild.wordpress.com/2014/09/20/bill-johnson-quotes/

Pray this with me:

Jesus, I thank You for making me righteous and holy, not by any work of my hands or flesh, but by Your finished work on the Cross. I declare and decree that every molecule of my entire being, in all its forms, is continually yielding to the righteousness of God ALREADY IN ME and is transforming me to manifest outwardly what God has already made me to be inwardly, in Jesus' Name! I declare and decree that I am immovable in my trust in what God has said and done, which is trust in His character. I declare that my righteousness was a gift from the Lord Jesus and is the power continuously at work in me as I yield more fully to Him. As I renew my mind and influence my heart, the salvation already in my spirit as one who is RIGHTEOUS is expanding to my soul and body in all of its parts, and to the world around me.

I do not need to become more righteous. In my spirit, I am as righteous as I can possibly be. I have always been righteous. My righteousness is, always has been, and always will be the righteousness of Christ. He has always seen and continues to see and love my heart, which is gold to Him. I tell failure that you have no place in my heart! I declare and decree that Jesus is continually healing my heart.

According to Your Word, Jesus, I AM A NEW CREATION, TOTALLY NEW, AND FAILURE HAS NO RIGHT TO TELL ME WHO I AM! I AM HOLY and RIGHTEOUS, and MY LIFE MANIFESTS RIGHTEOUSNESS BECAUSE I AM A TOTALLY NEW CREATION.

I declare and decree that the Spirit that raised Christ from the dead has raised me into newness of life. His victories are my victories, His anointing is my anointing, His inheritance is my inheritance, and His position in God is my position in

God in Christ Jesus. MY SPIRIT IS COMPLETELY LIBERATED TO HAVE DOMINION OVER MY SOUL AND BODY, IN JESUS' NAME!

DAY 11

Love Wins

"Some of you were once like that. But you were cleansed; you were made holy; you were made right with God by calling on the name of the Lord Jesus Christ and by the Spirit of our God."

-NLT, 1 Cor. 6:11

Every semester in my Bible Literature class, I get a new crop of students—mostly churched Generation Z (although I began with Millennials), with a handful of non-believers and seekers. The latter makes the class interesting because they always come with good questions. They don't have a religious filter (you've already heard some of my stories in an earlier chapter). Honestly, the classes' popularity is because the kids are drawn to me, and students know what they get with me—a teacher who truly loves them and is also a radical believer in Jesus.

Within my purview—at a public school in the Deep South—I have preached the Gospel in every context permissible and in some that were considered borderline. I have consistently pursued students with the experiential truth of who God is and called them forth into their destinies. I have lived boldly before them as a living example of what it means to present Jesus to the generation. I have poured out my life and heart without reservation, taking every opportunity I could, both inside and outside the classroom. To that end, I have fought an excellent fight.

As I have been intimately engaged with young people for over 20 years, I have become deeply convinced that this generation and the one coming behind them are embroiled in a crisis of faith of epic proportions. My students who grew up in youth groups and learned how to "look good" and "be good" on some level are as entrenched in the fluid sexuality mindset as the rest of the culture around them. I am also painfully aware of how entangled they are in their struggles with pornography, which is one of the most significant strategies of the enemy to hijack our youths' God-given sexuality and their ability to experience true intimacy. The only truth that some of my students embrace is divorced from a living faith and does not impose any moral limitations on behavior. Truth, in this generation, is not seen as something universal, but rather the product of one's experiences, making everyone's individual "truth" valid and "The Truth" null and void. This is not a judgment against them at all. I do not expect anyone who has a significant identity gap and doesn't know who they are in Jesus to be able to resist the strong pull of this cultural current. Not without something shifting on the inside of them.

Every year, I give the students journal assignments, and I make room for them to ask questions about any topic relevant to Christianity that they would like, and then use their questions to lead our discussions. Inevitably, within the first three days of class, a student wants to know what God thinks about sex, homosexuality in particular, and drug use. I always ask them what kind of answer they want. Do they want the Bible "literature" answer or the answer I would give as a believer and pastor? They always opt for the latter. One day, a young lady asked me, "If two young people, one straight, the other who acted and felt gay, and both had a relationship with

Jesus, got hit by a bus and tragically killed – where would they go, heaven or hell…?" I would rephrase and then confirm that's what they're asking me. I ask the class if they want my "pastor" answer to this question. Unanimously, they say "yes."

Taking a deep breath, I say "Ok, then." Some would think that I would be enthusiastic about this opportunity, and yes, on a level I am. But I am also keenly aware of what they are asking me to do and what it will look like when I give my extended answer. One of the most challenging things that we as Christian leaders are compelled to do to serve this generation well is to tell the Truth boldly – even if it isn't the answer they want to hear. More importantly, we have to tell the WHOLE truth, which means acknowledging our failure to love people who struggle in a way that conveys the heart of the Father. If we tell the part they want to hear without telling them the part that cuts across this culture of fluid sexuality, we're not helping. If we don't acknowledge the places where the church hasn't handled messy people well, we lose any voice we have with the generation.

My first response to the question that I knew would settle a few hearts before I continued was to repeat the questions and give them one of my own. So, I said, "If two young people, one who was straight, the other who felt and acted gay, both had a genuine relationship with Jesus and got hit by a bus and tragically killed – where would they go, heaven or hell? That's what you're asking me, right?" (Of course, everything is about the heart, so it's not always that simple. But is there a particular sin that sends someone straight to hell? How about adultery? Murder, maybe? That might be a problem for King David or even Moses.) The girl affirmed, and I answered, "Heaven."

For the next question, I volunteered because I knew it

was burning in their hearts, and I could see the question in their faces. I said, "You want me to tell you whether I think homosexuals are born that way or not." Their nods were the answer—second big breath.

I explained that "feeling" a certain way is not a true indicator of a sexuality that is designed that way by God, because our bodies can respond to a lot of things sexually without actually determining who we are and who we're created to be. God created mankind in His image. He was very intentional about creating male and female and giving them the command to "be fruitful and multiply." The two are of the same flesh but are also unique and correspond to one another in their design. There is relational fulfillment that can only be fully understood and experienced in the context that He created— marriage between a man and woman. That being true, we as a church have failed to love those who struggle in their sexuality and have often added to their shame because of how we have depicted sin—with some sins having greater shame than others.

It is true that not every sin is equal in terms of the consequences they produce—many which are reaped through the relational and sexual quagmire that comes when engaging with the sin. By stigmatizing and adding more shame to the sin of homosexuality, we transfer the shame of our own brokenness and addiction from ourselves to another whose sin looks "worse" than mine and, therefore, make our own sin more acceptable. We relegate the sin of homosexuality or any other aberrant form of sexual expression to the detestable and profane. But we forget who Jesus associated with while here on earth. Simon the Pharisee was appalled at Jesus' association with a prostitute, but in her ruined state, no expression of love and gratitude was too much for the Savior. Her delivery was messy, but it was indicative of how undone she was and how desperate she was to be forgiven, loved, accepted, and restored as a woman.

Our projection of shame in order to justify our own places of brokenness has made our voice irrelevant to a generation who freely acknowledges their own train wreck but shows acceptance to those who are different. That acceptance may be a bit skewed, but they will not be won over by being religious and judgmental.

I already used the example of holding ten perfect drinking glasses up and dropping them all from the same height. They all break, but they break differently. Some may split into three distinct pieces; others may shatter into a million pieces; still, others may shatter in a distinct pattern, and others break in non-descript ways. They are all broken. So, the only remedy for every broken "glass" is love. Love is the only thing that transforms. Judgment and shame become evil forces in the hands of the self-righteous. Ironically, the self-righteous and destitute are both transformed by the same Love — but the latter tend to find it quicker.

To redeem our relevance and place in this generation and come alongside as fathers and mothers in the faith, love must be our banner. We must love the broken and make that our only agenda, leaving Jesus to do the work that only He can do. Only when we can also see ourselves as one of the broken glasses will our walls of judgment fall, and we will see ourselves and others rightly. That is not to say that there is not a right and wrong, or that sin doesn't matter. It does. But how we win those caught in its bondage also matters. We have to learn what it means to speak the truth in love, without fear or judgment.

There is a changing of the guard in the Body of Christ,

and the champions of this next era will be bold lovers of both truth AND people. Our love will be contagious and transformative, as God inhabits the relational weakness in so many in our culture. Their attempts at finding love in detached and illegitimate forms of relating—whether it be through a pornographic image on a screen or fluid sexual encounters—have left them empty even while they scramble to up the ante.

There is a clarion call for the mothers and fathers in the faith to demonstrate real love and to mentor those coming up behind us, while simultaneously changing the atmosphere of the church in the places where there has been a deficit of love and grace.

Pray this with me:

Firstly, I come out of agreement with every lie about my sexuality, gender, and identity that I have allowed to shape how I see myself. I break them now in the name of Jesus. I come out of my position of looking to the creature to tell me who I am, and I look up You, my Creator, giving You permission to name me aright. I lay down my judgment of people and the many ways they sin in their efforts to fill the gap that only You can fill. Help me to see the Gold that You have put in them and make me a miner of that Gold. Help me to be an instrument to launch them into their destinies and promised futures in You. I choose to see only You in Your Creation, Lord. Make me a vessel of mercy and love as I also receive that same mercy and love from You. I will freely give away all You have and continue to give to me. In Jesus' Name. Amen!

DAY 12

Lost in Yonkers

"Did you ever notice there's something wrong with everyone on Pop's side of the family?"

-COOLIDGE, 1993, LOST IN YONKERS[14]

I love certain movies, particularly those that highlight the foibles of our humanity and paint a picture of redemption. Movies can be windows to the soul because the truth they convey does not clobber us in a frontal assault. Instead, it sneaks around our heart's fortifications and defenses, catching us by surprise. A truth that we may not hear in all the ways God has attempted to deliver it before suddenly comes as an epiphany as we laugh, cry, and fully engage with the story and characters depicted on the screen.

Lost in Yonkers is comical yet piercingly powerful in its depiction of a dysfunctional Jewish family in 1942 during WWII in Yonkers, New York. The matriarch of the family is a German Jew, mother, and grandmother who walks with a limp after having a horse fall on her foot, causing her daily pain—for which she has never taken as much as an aspirin.

After the death of two children early in life and the hardships of life and a nation at war, she has learned that to be tough like "steel" enables one to survive in this world. In

---

[14] Coolidge, M. (Director). (1993). Lost in Yonkers [Film]. Columbia Pictures.

Grandma's words, when her youngest daughter Bella asks her how she became this way, she explains, "The year Aaron died...I closed off from everybody [her children] ...from you and Louie...from Gert and Eddie. I lost Rose, then Aaron, and I stopped feeling because I couldn't stand losing anymore...." (Coolidge, 1993). Her "steeliness" makes her cold—impervious to emotion. Bound in her shame, she is incapable of demonstrating love to her four dysfunctional children. Jay, the older grandson, enlightens us when he says, "Did you ever notice there's something wrong with everyone on Pop's side of the family?" Uncle Louie is a henchman or "bagman," Aunt Gert can't breathe right because her mother wrecks her nerves. Bella is like a "child" in a grown woman's body, who should have gone to "the home." Eddie, the father of grandma's two grandsons, Jay, and Arthur, is characterized as spineless and terrified of his grandmother, who once chained him to the heat radiator as a child.

The central theme is about children born into a tragic and grossly dysfunctional family in 1942 and how they all respond to what happened. In a climactic scene after Bella tries to ask her mother's permission to get married and "have babies" who would not be like steel, Momma, from her self-justified position, tells Bella, "Stay a child, Bella, and be glad that's how God made you," and she walks away in deafening silence.

Exasperated from trying to pull blood from a hard, cold turnip, Bella shrieks, "Thieves and sick little girls, that what you have, Momma ...Only God didn't make them that way. You did!" Even today, after seeing the movie a hundred times, a shout thunders forth from me in audacious agreement. Bella has triumphed in naming the shame and core problem— Momma's frozen soul. As a classic narcissist and essential sociopath, Momma epitomizes what radical self-centeredness looks like as she retreats into herself — never to offer an apology, never to change even for the sake of the relationship. Everyone must tip-toe around her and relate to her on her terms alone — a tragically flawed woman who the viewer can't help but feel compassion for.

Later in the movie, Bella gets the grit and motivation to walk away from her mother's control, and she starts a new life in Florida. And we are left pondering all the things that have changed for her as she stops being a victim and takes charge of her own life. As painful as it is to extricate ourselves from a relationship where the other person refuses to let the Love of God melt their icy heart, sometimes we just must.

We can't make decisions for others, but we do have to decide how we will respond to them and how we will move forward with our own lives. We must see things from a much higher plane, getting God's perspective. We must always hold to the fact that nothing is lost in the Kingdom of God. Nothing. Everything that has happened to you, everything you have done, every place of regret, every place of failure, every place of lost hope, and every place of loss, coupled with your responses to what happened, have made you who you are today. To come out of shame is to bless the darkest parts of your story, making peace with them knowing God was there, God is good, and He redeems absolutely everything. That's how the economy of the Kingdom of Heaven functions. He is always moving in the unseen, the past, the present, and the future. He has missed nothing. The key to apprehending His redemption is in our declaration and knowing that HE IS GOOD. When we declare His goodness, we break the power of shame which says we are hopelessly flawed, and God brands us indelibly as His alone.

Pray this with me:

Lord, I declare that You are good no matter what my heart or head tell me. I ask You to do what only You can do — change this stony heart of mine, making it soft and responsive to every whisper that comes from Your mouth. I want to hear you more clearly. I choose to listen to only Your voice telling me who I am. I have given the keys to my heart to another, permitting them to tell me who I am — affirming a false identity. I repent — I change my mind — and give those keys to You. Father, remove the stones in my heart so that I can feel the sheer force of Love as You penetrate my very soul. Integrate every part of me that I have given to another, making me whole and complete in You alone. Show me how much You love me, and I declare that my heart will respond in agreement with Your Truth. In Jesus' Name. Amen.

DAY 13

Sickness Minus Shame

"The Spirit of the Lord is on me, because he has anointed me to proclaim good news to the poor. He has sent me to proclaim freedom for the prisoners and recovery of sight for the blind, to set the oppressed free."

-*NIV*, LUKE 4:18

Jesus spent His ministry on earth healing the sick, casting out demons, and raising the dead. He proclaimed the "...the Kingdom of God is at hand..." (*NIV*, Mark 1:15) and then He proceeded to demonstrate the works of the Kingdom. The proclamation and demonstration of the Kingdom were never meant to be divorced from each other. So often, particularly in Western Christianity, we are too cerebral for our own good — knowing well the truth of God's word, but naïve in experiencing His power, Spirit, and ways.

The late John Wimber[15] of the Vineyard church planting movement in the '80s challenged believers to go out and pray for people who need healing. His conviction was if every believer went out and prayed for a hundred people, they would

---

[15] "John Wimber, leader of the Vineyard movement in his lifetime, impacted the lives of thousands across the globe – and was used by God to renew the spiritual life of the 20th and 21st century Church (John Wimber, n.d.)." Retrieved from https://vineyardusa.org/about/john-wimber/

begin to see somebody get healed. Wimber led a movement in the church that was marked by intimate worship and power ministry—healing as evangelism. Like most of us, he struggled to understand the mystery of why not everyone gets healed. But he worked from the premise that God is good, and healing was always part of the banqueting table He laid before His Bride (part of the atonement). He was a huge catalyst in the resurrection of power ministry in the church—signs, wonders, and miracles.

Many avoid healing as one of the tenants of salvation partly out of ignorance, partly from a place of shame. Shame says, "I am not enough." Shame says, "we are just paupers in the Kingdom—sinners save by grace, and the most we can hope for in life is to survive it and then escape to Heaven." Jesus commissioned His disciples to bring Heaven to Earth and empowered them as carriers of the Kingdom. Disciples—that means us. Shame, however, keeps us bound to religion, and religion is tethered to the law. For those who value behavior management over freedom in the spirit, the law is wielded to keep everyone looking good but not alive to Holy Spirit. Shame says, "I am not enough to be trusted with the oracles of God, the works of the Kingdom, or supernatural encounters. Shame whispers, "God may have done that in this or that extreme situation for a particular person, but He doesn't do that today— we have all we need in the Bible. The Word divorced from the Spirit of God is good literature.

As Sid Roth said to the students in my classroom, "The Bible is a supernatural book." It is supernatural because the Holy Spirit is infused in the words on the page. He hovers over His promises, beckoning us to believe and shout our declaration of Truth from the mountaintops. He invites us to put Him to the test so that He can show us what a Faithful,

Good God He is. And while He longs to show us who He is, He doesn't actually need to prove anything. He is compelled by unfathomable love and compassion.

The other aspect of shame that we encounter in healing the sick is in the humanity of those we are privileged to pray for. Because God holds the right to mystery, He elicits our trust in His goodness. We trust that His ways are higher than ours and believe that we are HUGE on HIS map. We are also complex, and there are many factors in healing, including soul wounds and the individual's will and choices. As my wife says, "When we are in Him, we are safe, regardless of what the process looks like." We must know that just because every person does not get healed, we never throw in the towel, lying down in our shame. But we stand upright, faces burning, and eyes fixed on the Crucified and Resurrected One who we love, adore, and know both as Father and Friend. We move forward, knowing that as painful as it is when healing isn't manifested in some, many ARE healed. Still others make their transition to Heaven with the door knocker in their hand, knuckles bloodied, and NOTHING IS MISSED by the KING OF HEAVEN and EARTH. His recompense for that which has been lost in any arena is exponential.

Heaven doesn't do "tit for tat," we win one—we lose one. Heaven has recorded every drop of blood by a martyr, every fight for life and healing that ended in temporary death, every devastation, every loss of fortune, reputation, and broken relationship. Heaven's math is so much better because it is always "exceedingly abundantly above all that we can ask or think," (NKJV, Eph. 3:20).

Restoration and reconciling all things to Christ will most likely look different from what we imagine. But when it comes, it will excite us beyond measure as the grand realization hits us—that God's recompense had everything to do with the desires of the heart—even when I didn't know my own heart yet. Even when I had to have an encounter so that I could have an encounter that opened my eyes us up to the Grand Convergence that has been the theme of every thread woven into the tapestry of my life. Always, in retrospect, we see. On the front end, we trust, cling, believe and persevere even in the darkest hours, knowing that we will see His goodness in the land of the living.

Pray this with me:

Lord, I lay down the shame that tells me that healing couldn't possibly be part of the atonement. I lay down the shame that says that everyone can be healed — except me. Lord, I welcome every paradigm shift that needs to come for me to "see." Bring the encounter with You that prepares me for the next encounter so that I am continuously being transformed by You. I declare that You are good, Lord, even when I do not understand why You do things the way You do. I choose to trust and cling to you on this end, knowing that when I look back at this time in my life, I will see and understand more. I want the blessing and honor of knowing You as a friend with whom You share Your secrets. I want the gift of being a son or daughter who trusts the Unseen Real.

DAY 14

Shame in Disappointment

'In these porticoes lay a great number of people who were sick, blind, lame, withered, [waiting for the stirring of the water; for an angel of the Lord went down into the pool at appointed seasons and stirred up the water; the first one to go in after the water was stirred was healed of his disease.] There was a certain man there who had been ill for thirty-eight years. When Jesus noticed him lying there [helpless], knowing that he had been in that condition a long time, He said to him, "Do you want to get well?" The invalid answered, "Sir, I have no one to put me in the pool when the water is stirred up, and while I am coming [to get into it myself], someone else steps down ahead of me." So, Jesus said to him, "Get up; pick up your pallet and walk." Immediately the man was healed and recovered his strength, and picked up his pallet and walked.'

-AMP, JOHN 5:3-9, [*EMPHASIS MINE*]

Shame can be experienced as discouragement when defeat is perceived as temporary, or shame may gain opportunity by failure to attain whatever goal has been set on a particular attempt to accomplish something.[16] It often builds

---

[16] Kaufman, G. (1993). The psychology of shame: Theory and treatment of shame- based syndromes. London: Routledge.

upon itself, becoming established deep in our souls.

Shame takes advantage when hope has been deferred. The biblical concept is, "Hope deferred makes the heart sick, but a desire fulfilled is a tree of life" (*ESV*, Prov. 13:21). Our experiences with great disappointment and discouragement often make the heart sick, even when our minds can rationalize and minimize these events in our attempt to find peace. The heart remembers every affliction, and our subconscious stores these events like fragmented data that is always there on the hard drive but not always easily detected at first scan.

In this passage, Jesus already knew the condition of the man was chronic, that he had been stuck in the familiarity of only knowing himself as lame, both physically and metaphorically. Many times, when reading this passage, I mused over why Jesus asked this man if he wanted to get well. My rational mind said, "Of course, he does; the man's been sick forever—look at him, he can't even get the help he needs when the angel comes to stir the waters of the pool!" I always marveled at the man's response to the question: "Sir, I have no one to put me in the pool when the water is stirred up, and while I am coming [to get into it myself], someone else steps down ahead of me." It sounds like he is making an excuse and ignoring the question!

The wisdom shown in Jesus' use of the question comes from His knowledge of the human heart. What happens when failure, discouragement, and extended seasons of disappointment have been our only experiences (or at least that has been our perception)? How defective, wrong, broken, and unloved we often feel when our dreams crash and burn.

Bill Johnson of Bethel Church in Redding, California, has repeatedly said that the biggest problem in Christendom today is the underlying belief that God is not good. Most Christians, on hearing that, would scoff and bristle in false pride in our attempt to escape the shame of its truth in our hearts. We don't say it out loud, but our heart confirms that it is true if we allow the Holy Spirit to plumb its depths.

The terror of the unfamiliar often keeps us in bondage to that which we know. This man had only known sickness and defeat. As an invalid, every attempt he made to step into the pool was cut short by others who were either more mobile or who had more help. Someone always beat him there. Perhaps he had listened to a plethora of "Hallelujahs" and celebrations as one after another left the portico of Bethesda healed, whole, and with hope restored. The anger and rage eventually turned inward as self-contempt and depression, as the sting of injustice penetrated and poisoned his long-lost hope, leaving him a bitter man. At what point had he let despair become the only food for his soul?

Jesus did not allow him to recount his experiences of repeated failure to get healed, nor did He shame him because he was not healed or had been there so long. He didn't even tell him that he apparently didn't have the faith to be healed.
Most of the shame that we experience when we do not see our breakthrough in any area comes from either ourselves or those closest to us.

As Christians, we often foist the shame of our failure and unbelief onto those who have been beaten up and left for dead in the church because the pain of our own disappointment and the resultant shame is too much to bear. Jesus told this man, "Get up; pick up your pallet and walk," and "Immediately the man was healed and recovered his strength, and picked up his pallet and walked" (*AMP*, John 5:8-9, italics added).

Jeremiah 17:9 says, "The heart is deceitful above all things and beyond cure. Who can understand it?" (*NIV*).

Sometimes in the daily grind of doing life, I do not get the time to reflect and process what is in my heart, especially when navigating through multiple storms simultaneously. The challenge to slow down and listen to my heart, allowing the Holy Spirit total access, can be formidable. Sometimes, I need to encounter God first to prepare me for another encounter with God that is transformative.

In other words, I need to put myself in the atmosphere, whether it be a church meeting, a conference, my own secret place, or in the company of those who know how to listen well, and pray from that well. We cannot see what we cannot see until we see it. Initial encounters with God, where we pull aside and give God room to penetrate our being, can dislodge and unearth stones in the soil that we were not aware were there, enabling us to hear and see something new. One encounter sets the stage for the next.

Pray this with me:

Father, I thank You that You are Grand Pursuer of my heart and that You never sleep, slumber, or allow all that is in me to go unnoticed. I want to encounter You in ways that jump-start my heart, allowing You further and greater access. Every place where I have knowingly or unknowingly harbored a lie in my heart, I ask You to unearth it, bring it to light so that I can repent for my wrong way of thinking about who You are. You are a Good, Good, Father, and You only want what is good for me. I thank You, Lord, that I am HUGE on Your map and that Your pursuit of me enables me to follow hard after you. Apart from Your Grand Initiative, I would forever flounder — lost, afraid, and unhealed. Come and get me, Holy Spirit! I am Yours, and Yours Alone. (Stop and listen to what He speaks to your heart. Let Him remove the boulders of disappointment from your soul as He loves on you). In Jesus' name. Amen.

DAY 15

Shame Makes Us Run

"My frame was not hidden from you when I was made in the secret place, when I was woven together in the depths of the earth."

-NIV, PSALM 139:15

hame is not always conscious. Sometimes it is like ingesting poison, and its toxicity leavens the whole lump of our being, permeating quietly, unnoticed in the background. The lens through which we view life becomes jaded, skewed, always looking for meaning and identity from the created rather than the Creator, and in our distorted perceptions, we become toxic to ourselves and to those around us.

High school was a disaster for me. It was one of the most alienating, discombobulating experiences of my life. My deep sense of "something is really wrong with me" colored my world—a world painted with the brushes of rejection, abandonment, and self-loathing. I did not have any consistent friends. I did not fit into any group, and I was addicted to getting attention in any way that I could.

I was the clown—the one that teachers dreaded would blurt out the unthinkable. A clown is great fun in the moment, but the clown always walks away with the fallout—dejected, alone, and facing who knows what kinds of bad consequences. There is pain and darkness beneath that mask.

The problem with deep shame is that it often goes

incognito, causing great destruction as it informs the decisions we make, the actions we take, the thoughts we think, and the emotions we feel—all behind the scenes. So hidden, it never gets diagnosed, labeled, or healed, even as it compels us from one self-destructive fiasco to the next. Before we know it, we are in a self-perpetuating cycle, facing the same devastating results in every part of our lives. The shame cycle must be interrupted, dismantled piece by piece, and rendered null and void. Without interruption, shame would drive us to the edge of the cliff and thrust us over into tragedy where we never know what real love is, the reason we exist, or what life would look like when we are fully awakened to our true selves.

This is where Jesus comes in. He is the only one who can deliver us from the hell of ourselves because He took all our shame and humiliation as He hung naked on the Cross. He took it all so that we would be made the manifest sons and daughters of the King of the Universe when He decisively pulverized the enemy and made him a public spectacle. We were made to bring Heaven to Earth, destroying the works of the evil one, setting captives free, releasing prisoners to new LIFE.

In my senior year of high school, I was out of control, desperately looking for anyone to think I was cool, one of the gang, part of the human race called teenagers. One day when my mother gave me her car to drive to school, I immediately gathered a group of people that I didn't even know well to come to my house for drinks and pizza. I prostituted myself (figuratively speaking), literally paying for the illusion of having friends, being part of the gang. After I hung up the phone from ordering the pizza, I did something very foolish. I said, "Who wants to go pick up the pizza?" and I handed car keys to the first taker. The minute he drove off with my mother's car, I knew. The large pit in my stomach and the sledgehammer pounding my chest screamed, "What have you done?!"

When the kid came back, I collapsed in a hysterical wail, panicking because the entire driver's side of the car was bashed in, so much so that the whole vehicle looked bent. Frantically, I tried to find out what happened. The kid and the friend that went with him swore up and down that another driver wrongfully hit them. As I got closer to the car, the bark embedded in the side of the vehicle betrayed them. They had wrapped my mother's new car around a massive tree as they attempted to round a corner going 80 miles an hour in a residential street near my house.

The only thing I knew in the moments that followed was I could not face my mother, so I made another extremely foolish decision. I found the nearest person to a friend that I could, a kid who wasn't happy with his father's strict rules, and convinced him to run away with me. We gathered every bit of money we could find or steal from our parents' houses and took off in my orange VW bug.

Writing this now, I am confronted with how unstable I was in those days in high school—how surreal the whole debacle was, what a string of poor, shame-based decisions I made then. I have long ago been healed of many of those places in my soul, but I can still remember the deep inner loneliness. Being alone and being lonely are two very different things. Being alone can be a time for introspection and healthy reflection. I am much better at being alone now without panic rising in me, without that sense of deep inner loneliness. Inner loneliness is something that is always there even when surrounded by people who love us well. It is that inner loneliness that can be dangerous for many of us and needs to be healed. That inner loneliness isn't just loneliness. It has another name — SHAME.

Shame is the grand separator and isolator. It's the labyrinth of emotions, thoughts, and vague feelings of restlessness that can be shoved to the background in frenetic busyness but whose pang is felt the most when we are alone. This pang called Shame must meet Jesus face to face, must touch Him, be held by Him, be encountered by Him, must be swallowed up IN HIM. If not, like Cain, it will compel us to ease it with anything we can find. Today, we have named the pang. Naming it gives us great power over it, but naming it alone is not enough. The pang in my chest must be filled with the only One who can heal it — His name is Jesus.

Pray this with me:

Jesus, I cannot even begin to wrap my head around some of the things in my heart that propel me into places of loneliness and isolation, feeding my addictions in an attempt to soothe it. I thank You that I do not have to know the answer, get it right, or make something happen. All I have to do is come to You. Lord, I acknowledge that this pang called shame has been a big part of my heart and I repent for trying to find life in restlessness and the frenetic energy I expend in "doing." Deliver me from "doing" and liberate me to "be," so that I am fully present to You, others, and myself. Holy Spirit, I permit You to access my heart, to teach me how to connect to You in more significant ways—ways that heal my loneliness and propel me further into You. I thank You that I am not left to myself to figure it out or get it all right. You are with me. You and I are One. Jesus, show me where You are RIGHT NOW in my picture, in my life, in my room. Your presence is my comfort and fills the lonely places. Come into them now. I open the door wide to You so You can access every part of my soul. I am never alone!! Thank You, Jesus!

DAY 16

Quick Trip Back to the Garden

"Of all the wild creatures the Eternal God had created, the serpent was the craftiest.
***Serpent** (to the woman): Is it true that God has forbidden you to eat fruits from the trees of the garden?*
***Eve:** No, serpent. God said we are free to eat the fruit from the trees in the garden. We are granted access to any variety and all amounts of fruit with one exception: the fruit from the tree found in the center of the garden. God instructed us not to eat or touch the fruit of that tree, or we would die.*
***Serpent:** Die? No, you'll not die. God is playing games with you. The truth is that God knows the day you eat the fruit from that tree you will awaken something powerful in you and become like Him: possessing knowledge of both good and evil.*
The woman approached the tree, eyed its fruit, and coveted its mouth-watering, wisdom-granting beauty. She plucked a fruit from the tree and ate. She then offered the fruit to her husband who was close by, and he ate as well. Suddenly their eyes were opened to a reality previously unknown. For the first time, they sensed their vulnerability and rushed to hide their naked bodies, stitching fig leaves into crude loincloths. Then they heard the sound of the Eternal God walking in the cool misting shadows of the garden. The man and his wife took cover among the trees and hid from the Eternal God."

-THE VOICE BIBLE, GEN. 3:1-6

One of the most significant impacts of the Fall of man and a consequence of sin is our descent into shame. The church's historic hyper-focus on "sin" has been about managing behavior — and this emphasis has kept us eating from the Tree of the Knowledge of Good and Evil. This fuels shame because it keeps us focused on sin — and you become what you focus on. True freedom from sin comes as a result of a secured identity in Christ and greater awareness of our union with Him. Ironically, when the church hyper-focuses on sin, its main goal is to promote "Christian" behavior, not our oneness with Christ. In Jesus' most magnificent rant against the Pharisees in Matthew 23 (*NLT*), He says:

> *"They crush people with unbearable religious demands..." (v. 4).*
> *"Everything they do is for show..." (v. 5).*
> *"...Hypocrites! For you shut the door of the Kingdom of Heaven in people's faces. You won't go in yourselves, and you don't let others enter either," (v. 13).*
> *"Outwardly you look like righteous people, but inwardly your hearts are filled with hypocrisy and lawlessness," (v. 28).*

One of the most significant impacts of the Fall of man and a consequence of sin is our descent into shame. The church's historic hyper-focus on "sin" has been about managing behavior — and this emphasis has kept us eating from the Tree of the Knowledge of Good and Evil. This fuels shame because it keeps us focused on sin — and you become what you focus on. True freedom from sin comes as a result of a secured identity in Christ and greater awareness of our union with Him. Ironically, when the church hyper-focuses on sin, its main goal is to promote "Christian" behavior, not our oneness with

Christ. In Jesus' most magnificent rant against the Pharisees in Matthew 23 (*NLT*), He says: "They crush people with unbearable religious demands..." (v. 4). "Everything they do is for show..." (v. 5). "...Hypocrites! For you shut the door of the Kingdom of Heaven in people's faces. You won't go in yourselves, and you don't let others enter either," (v. 13). "Outwardly you look like righteous people, but inwardly your hearts are filled with hypocrisy and lawlessness," (v. 28).

As we have talked about throughout this devotional, shame is either turned inward as self-contempt or projected outward as other-centered contempt, self-righteousness, and judgment. Jesus calls the Pharisees out for their self-righteous hypocrisy, lawlessness, and for blockading the door to the Kingdom of Heaven. The Pharisees had a massive investment in looking good on the outside and projecting their shame and false superiority on the followers of Jesus. For them, control was essential. While flaunting their seemingly righteous deeds, their lawless and narcissistic hearts sought to annihilate their opposition. I always make a joke about not rejecting a narcissist because they will not just come back at you—they will seek to annihilate you, fueled by their rage and need for absolute revenge. They do not do rejection well.

The Pharisaic spirit is married to shame and is antithetical to the work of the Holy Spirit, who brings release and freedom from our futile attempts at managing our lives and looking good. We are culturally entrenched in shame because of the fragmentation of the family unit and its consequential dysfunction. This disintegration of the nuclear family has fueled the exponential growth of shame in the soul of a generation. The parable of the leaven in the bread is a good analogy for how shame penetrates, grows, and works itself through the entire lump of dough. In saying this, I am not judging the various families out there in their brokenness. Compassion, grace, and mercy are still the tools of the Kingdom, and the power of the Resurrection undoes every work of the evil one. There is not anything that the Cross cannot cancel. Nothing is irreversible in the Kingdom of God.

The Blood of Jesus utterly dismantles shame at its core.

In the 1980's, I stumbled into a small church that was part of the Vineyard led by John Wimber. I met the pastor, Denny Strickland, who later married me both times (the second time to the love of my life who I have been married to for almost 25 years). For me as an Indiana University student on fire for Jesus, walking into that church and meeting Denny (who has since joined my cloud of witnesses) was as providential and life changing as it gets.

In every season in history, there are movements, revivals, and emphases on various aspects of the ministry of the Holy Spirit that get highlighted — some of them simultaneously. One thing that God was doing in the 1980s and '90s was healing our souls. There was an anointing for God to heal deep rifts in people's hearts and free them from the bondage that they experienced because of traumas of the past that festered under the surface. Personally, I was pretty unhinged in my early 20's. I was grieving the abandonment of a father in the first years of my life, and forgiving profound violations from physical, emotional, and sexual abuse at the hand of my biological father. As I allowed the Holy Spirit to plumb the depths of my being, He reached into places that felt hollowed out and pulled death up and out me, placing it into the cross. His arm was not too short for me.

To give you snapshot of the kind of anointing that made healing souls easy at that time, I'll share one of many encounters at church on Sunday morning. The worship was contemporary — intimate Vineyard worship songs which were a bit haphazard and rough on a technical front this particular morning. Yet what would seem to a seasoned worship leader to be a fairly crude version of a worship set, played without rehearsal, was alive and penetrating when the Holy Spirit was breathing on it.

Worship was an encounter with God where one lingered, not a quick set of songs as a prelude to a message. One morning after worship, three minutes into the message, Denny pulled his granny readers down to the edge of his nose, pointed his finger at me, and under the unction of the Holy Spirit stopped and said, "Oh, and the Holy Spirit is going to visit you this morning, Scott." Ten minutes later, I was in a fetal position on the floor, wailing my guts out. Not at all contrived, deep loneliness and heart-wrenching grief were being healed.

I was freed from all kinds of shame through my mentor, Denny — whether in a service, or during one of many multi-hour chats — to ultimately be myself, and to bear my soul. I was safe. I...was...SAFE. And in that safety, there is healing. I have known few fathers in the faith who could create that sense of true safety that Denny did. He drew people who were like him, people who were real with him and each other, and they became my family. Having come from a broken home (no reflection on my mother and amazing adoptive father), I never knew that love and freedom without shame could ever look this good. If we want to participate in reconciling all things to Jesus and see our land healed, WE MUST BECOME THAT SAFE PLACE, where mercy triumphs over judgment and the sacred cows of the Pharisees in our midst are torn down.

There has never been a time in history when the need for community and family was as colossal as it is now. Yet, as we move further away from the nuclear family into fragmentation and dysfunction, shame is compounded and exponentially increases. As good as any modern family configuration can be, the original design of the family as a fundamental building block has become a construct of the past that we can no longer relate to.

Our redemption is found in the One who can undo every curse of the Fall—who can create beauty for the ashes that our lives and dreams became. The pendulum on broken relational structures has swung in one direction about as far as it can without becoming completely unhinged. How long do we have to ride the train of liberal progressiveness, which champions the very lawlessness that has gotten us where we are today? As we face the crumbling of our culture and society, we MUST see a revival in the land which by the power of the Holy Spirit can reset our moral compass. Jesus is always poised and ready to unleash the power of the Kingdom of God in the manifest sons and daughters of God that the very earth is groaning for. All He needs is a generation that will stand in the gap and say "YES." Let's give Him our individual and our corporate yes!

Pray this with me:

Lord, I ask you to deliver me from any place of striving in my own heart to "get it right" and manage my life and behavior instead of just spending time with You. Father, I am laying down my religion, and I am going after knowing You as a Father and a Friend. I want to know what it means to be fully loved by You, no matter what state I am in. I acknowledge that You are not distracted by my distractions—which are many. Holy Spirit, I ask that You awaken a sense of being in me—that awareness of my completeness and union with You. Awaken my spirit. Awaken my heart—even now. Awaken me to Your Love and still the restless activism in my heart. "Be still and know that I am God" (*NIV*, Ps. 46:10). Interrupt me with Your Love when I try too hard and show me how near You are to me. I choose You, Lord!

DAY 17

Modern Day Prodigals

"Am I ever going to get delivered? Will I be struggling with this garbage my whole life? How many times can I tick God off before He just dumps me?! I love Jesus, but I can't ever do the right thing to make him proud of me."

Years ago, I co-facilitated 24-week recovery groups for men and women who were dealing with every kind of sexual addiction you could think of and some that most of us cannot. We taught on a topic with the whole group and then split into men's and women's groups, where the conversation changed drastically. In the first part of these meetings, the men told the group how their week went. There were times when they told stories of defeat, having given in to their addictions, cycled through shame, and repeated the cycle. The shame in their eyes as their heads inevitably dropped, breaking eye contact, was tangible. Their desperation hung in the air, permeating the atmosphere with shame, discouragement, and hopelessness. Then, their heads would come slowly up as others joined into the uneasy chorus of humiliation.

Next came my part. After capturing all eyes in the room, I would say something like this, "Here's the deal—you are forgiven, and Jesus is present with you right now. He has never left you, never turned His head in disgust because of your broken humanity. Shame makes you feel defective, and it makes you want to hide because you don't think you are very lovable or desirable when you struggle with the same sin issue again and again. The place where the enemy wins is when he gets you to believe the lie that God has turned away from you — that somehow God is a dysfunctional parent. The most significant thing that enemy is after in the middle of the struggle is to shut down your voice. The lies that shame propagates serve the purpose of making us feel like we are shipwrecked, that we are an extra tough case for God, and He will eventually walk away shaking His head in disgust when He has had enough of me."

There are a couple of clips from the amazing and popular crowd-funded series on the story of Jesus and His disciples called "The Chosen" that depict this so well. One is from a scene when Mary Magdalene, who had already been sought out and delivered by Jesus, returned briefly to her old lifestyle because of her response to fresh trauma. Matthew and Simon went out to find her and when trying to convince her to return with them, she utters the following shame-filled statement: "He already fixed me once. And I broke again." Once she was brought back to face Jesus, she responded to Him, "I'm so ashamed. You redeemed me and I just threw it all away." Jesus' reply to her echoes loudly even now as I consider the ramifications. "Well, that's not much of a redemption if it can be lost in a day, is it?"[17] We would do well to pause there and let it sink in.

Two huge factors come into play when we minister to people whose addictive lifestyles have a history of shame-

---

[17] Jenkins, D. (2017-). The Chosen [Television series]. USA: VidAngel Studios.

empowered and self-destructive cycles. The first is the Word of God and the second is the Presence of the Holy Spirit. We need to speak truth to others and ourselves, calling forth the gold without highlighting the dross. The Word of God is living, and, to quote Sid Roth again, "It is a supernatural book." This means that every encounter with the Word of God—spoken, read, or meditated upon—yields fruit. It must. Nothing spoken comes back void, and nothing ingested in our spirit fails to impact. The soil of the heart either limits or exponentially increases the impact of the leaven of the Word in the lump of clay—in our spirit, soul, and body.

When working with those who have life-dominating, debilitating issues, who love Jesus but who are battle-worn in the struggle, the Word of God is the change agent. They (we) need to learn to declare the promises of God and to change negative self-talk through declarations of the Truth. Often, we must declare a truth that our hearts may not yet fully apprehend, but we do it in faith, knowing that our heart will eventually follow. The place where we can do damage and set people back in their progress is when we use the Word of God to shame those whose struggles are messy and make us uncomfortable. When we trivialize the application of the Word of God and elevate our mental assent to principles (our cerebral agreement with the Word devoid of the Spirit), we assign judgment and communicate the wrong message. This is shame-based religion—it renders the Word ineffectual in the lives of those to whom we minister.

Those who struggle in addiction, while longing for freedom, often stay trapped because the shame they experience in failure is compounded by religious shame. The Truth that we should be communicating to those who have long-standing issues with addictive lifestyles is that the ministry of the Word is constantly impacting their souls supernaturally. The Word divorced from the Spirit (the person of the Holy Spirit) of Compassion can cut them to shreds, leaving them bloodied and unhealed—as we walk away feeling smug and justified as a modern-day Pharisee. Knowing the Truth and delivering the Truth under the unction of the Holy Spirit tempered by Love are two radically different things. The latter frees to the uttermost. The Word must be demonstrated in the Presence of God as we teach others to mediate the Presence in their own lives. The Word delivered from our mouths is coupled with the rhema Word of the Spirit. Two words from the mouth of God to the ears of those having been shamed can transform their hearts in an instant. They not only hear the Word—they ENCOUNTER HIM.

Mediating the Presence of God changes our trajectory, our DNA, and even our brain chemistry, making the Word on the page the Word on Heavenly steroids. Our failure to mediate the Presence of the Holy Spirit in our ministry to those with life-dominating issues has left them defrauded. We have traded an Encounter with the Word for a Bible study and religious mandate to "shape up or ship out." The cognitive dissonance that one experiences between what they know to be true in God's word and their experience of that truth in their lives becomes the final nail in the coffin for many. They abdicate the church and a faith that feels delusional and bereft of power—the power needed to save them.

Truth is the Word, and that same Word is an encounter. This is a mystery, but it is a mystery that we continue to discover as we awaken to our UNION with Him—the knowing that we are not separate, but ONE. In our ONENESS, we ENCOUNTER LOVE, and our ENCOUNTER of LOVE transforms our hearts and repositions our perspective and our ability to see differently. As Presence-oriented creatures, we were created to live, move, and have our being IN HIM (Acts 17:28). Encounter is our NORM — not the exception or relegated to the few.

Pray this with me:

Jesus, You are the Word, You are a person, and You are my encounter with Love in this life. Cause me to know Love. Draw me, Holy Spirit, into a lifestyle of practicing Your Presence as One who is forever with me. You never leave me. You never hide. You are never caught off guard by my humanity. You are never put off by anything about me. You are not distracted because I am distracted. You are not waiting for me to get it together before You initiate with me. You love me, as I am, for who I am—the parts of me that I know, and the parts of me that I don't yet know. Any darkness in me is light to You. Jesus, I see what Your book says. Heal the rift between my head and my heart that my heart may fully know Your Love for me. Tell me what You think of me, and in so doing, replace my words of shame with Your words of love, acceptance, and promise. In Jesus' Name. Amen.

DAY 18

The Faith of a Child

'But Jesus said, "Let the children come to me.
Don't stop them! For the Kingdom of Heaven
belongs to those who are like these children."

-NLT, MATT. 19:14

When I was at Indiana University as an undergraduate, I was a devoted Christian—pure in my faith. I believed God could do anything. In my simplicity, I wanted to reach out to my college campus, and my idea was to have a worship session in one of the leading academic buildings. I went to my pastor and pitched my idea for outreach, and he saw my raw passion. He heartily agreed to help me do it. So, I printed up a flyer announcing the date and time for a worship event on campus in Ballantine Hall. I faithfully plastered the building with flyers, and our pastor brought a small worship team and a couple of other faithful members to support my efforts. I nervously looked at my watch and the empty room as the start time approached and felt my heart sink lower into my chest as no one came.

My pastor, Denny, pulled me from my slump and insisted that we go ahead with the worship event as planned—a valuable lesson in Kingdom ministry as well as a great entrepreneurial experience. He told me, "We never despise small beginnings." He was right. Whether this event would blossom into a future event or not, it was a start at penetrating the campus for Jesus. In the Kingdom of God, the most significant part we play in seeing Heaven come to earth is simply "showing up." Regardless of how we assess our performance or completion of our interpretation of the Father's heart or agenda in a matter, the Holy Spirit and the hosts of Heaven never waste an opportunity. When we show up, they show up and accomplish in the Unseen Real that which we may never be aware.

The Kingdom of Heaven in us is NEVER STAGNANT — it is ALWAYS dynamic. I know that in everything I do, all of the Kingdom of God is within me. I carry it, and wherever I go, and I assume that the very atmosphere changes when I show up. That is not a narcissistic statement. It is a 'Union with Jesus' statement. Denny knew that we moved Heaven and changed the atmosphere when we showed up at Ballantine Hall that day, and he wanted to model what it meant to "show up" and avail ourselves of the opportunity that Heaven presented. On the entrepreneurial front, it was a "completed" assignment, even if it feels like a failure.

As Heaven's entrepreneurs, collaborating to see creative strategies that further the Kingdom of God on earth, initiation is always celebrated. When we initiate with our words and actions, we frame up a reality that becomes palpable as we speak and act it into existence — again, and again, if need be — until we see the manifestation of what we have sown in the Unseen Real.

Denny taught me that day that it was okay to "fail" as I perceived it. But the even greater lesson was that in the Kingdom of God we CAN'T fail. Childlike faith is always rewarded. Instead of feeling shamed and defective because I didn't pull off the event I envisioned, I felt empowered and free to take risks. Denny recognized my child-like faith and simplicity of heart in my attempt to impact the campus for the sake of Christ. Too often, we employ our business model to all our initiatives, and in so doing, we deploy the shame that goes with perceived failure that aborts a Heavenly mission or a Kingdom lesson.

In a culture of shame, failure is not seen as an opportunity to learn through risk-taking but rather as a liability that must be managed. A religious environment that values the appearance of health rather than true spiritual health perpetuates the plight of the older, religious son in the parable of the Prodigal son. He was indignant at the sight of the party thrown for his brother and refused to participate, citing his complaint, "...Father, listen! How many years have I worked like a slave for you, performing every duty you've asked as a faithful son? And I've never once disobeyed you. But you've never thrown a party for me because of my faithfulness" Luke 15: 29, 30a (*TPT*).

His father reminds him that he has been by his side all along. This statement implies that everything that the father had was always available to him as a son, but he traded the relationship for works. He found himself full of contempt, foisting the shame of his failure to earn his father's affections on to his brother in his desperate appeal. "But look at [this son of yours]! He comes back after wasting your wealth on prostitutes and reckless living, and here you are throwing him a great feast to celebrate—for him!" (*TPT*, Luke 15: 30b).

Although the bigger "sinner," the Prodigal son was childlike in his repentance. Religion always finds child-like repentance to be an offense. It will also seek to highlight failure in an attempt to make the "messy one" with blatant sin the target of shame to sidestep the manifestation of their own shame in self-righteous arrogance and pride. Justified in their own eyes, they point the finger of judgment at the "sinner," condemning their child-like attempt to reconnect to love, compassion, and forgiveness. Sadly, they find no need to be forgiven themselves. Religion drives a hard bargain, demanding that we abandon our child-like response to Jesus in exchange for the heavy burden of keeping the outside of the cup spotless. At the same time, we inwardly fester in our alienation and separation from Love.

Pray this with me:

Jesus, I cannot deliver myself from my religious compulsion to get it right—to compel you to love me and approve of me. Deliver me from the hell of myself where I live in torment, desperate to be loved and know love, but uncertain how to get it. I choose to lay down the religion that I know is in me and to trust You to weed out the rest, making my heart pliable to Your love and Your initiation upon me. Draw me, Jesus, and I will follow. Touch my heart, and my heart will rise up into Your love. Show me what Love looks like and how much You love me, that my motivations will be birthed from love, not shame. Help me to be willing to take risks without fear, knowing that I can't fail when I stay close to You. In Jesus' Name, Amen.

DAY 19

Baptism and the God that Answers by Fire

"And you call upon the name of your god, and I will call upon the LORD, and the God who answers by fire, he is God. And all the people answered, 'It is well spoken.'"

-*ESV*, 1 KINGS 18:24

When my wife and I first went to the revival in Dawsonville, Georgia at Christ Fellowship Church, she was healed of breast cancer in the baptismal pool. I took three of my students with me to go experience it for themselves. In that season, the public school where I taught had skated the edge of revival a couple of times — and this was one of them. I had seen so many students and faculty healed and touched powerfully by God through the years (all before or after school, or during lunch, of course). In the sanctuary of my classroom, I had low-key prophesied to many of them, calling them into what they were created for. Basically, I was just telling them who they are without saying, "thus saith the Lord." Many had experienced the fire of God for the first time and had encounters with the Holy Spirit. Sometimes when you talk about Him, He just shows up. Of course, He's always there, but sometimes He's more 'tangibly' present.

My students were used to the idea that the fire of God showed up on them often in the classroom. But things were heating up in my room again, and I wanted some of the kids to experience the Fire in the Water in Dawsonville, Georgia. I knew from previous revivals that in the gathering stages, many get impartations that spark a revival in the city, state, or country they are returning to. As the desperate and hungry come to the altars of Fire, whether it be a physical altar or a fiery baptismal pool, Jesus always gives them more than they asked for. For many, they become fire starters, and the revival intensifies as the newly lit "walking revivals" scatter and carry the burning torch with them.

Dre, DJ, and Rhett, two African American students and, as I always affectionately called him, "one skinny little white boy", made our trip to Dawsonville. DJ was backing out at the last second because his mother feared that he would not take care of his body on the journey. He was born with Cystic Fibrosis and had struggled to breathe his whole life. His daily routine included breathing treatments, medications, and a special vest that shook his chest for several minutes to loosen the phlegm in his lungs so that through long fits of coughing and heaving, he could spit it up. As a natural-born athlete, he was forced to abandon all hope of playing basketball because it required too much breath.

In a holy texting fury, I texted his mother, a prophetic minister, and told her about my wife getting healed of stage three breast cancer in that water in Dawsonville. The "crying" emoticons flooded my screen as she simultaneously texted me and her son to tell him that he needed to go. She said to me that God had given her a promise that her son would be completely healed before he went to college. He was now a high school senior, and she acknowledged that she was not expecting his opportunity for healing to come in the baptismal revival package. But knowing God was working, she consented to let him go.

I had the honor of baptizing these guys with the pastor, Marty Darracott, who always ministers in the baptismal pool. The Fire of God hit all of us as we were standing and being interviewed before being submerged. The best part was falling backward into liquid Fire and the Presence of the Holy Spirit in the water. Dre felt the Fire of God on his feet before he even stepped into the pool and was completely disoriented in the Holy Ghost when he came up out of the water. The other two boys rose from the water, visibly shaken. They were caught off guard and arrested by the Fire of God, which they felt tangibly in the water.

What came after the baptism itself was the icing on this cake. A few hours after, when we were on our way to dinner, DJ said, "I can breathe; I feel like my chest literally expanded." Later, he told me that he felt the Fire of God burning in his chest for several hours after the baptism experience.

Dre didn't have a physical condition that needed to be healed, but he was violently apprehended in the water. Out of all of the photographs taken that night by the church's resident photographer, Dre's was the poignant picture of transformation. He told me the next day on our drive back that he felt the Fire of God in his chest all night long!

My "skinny white boy," Rhett, wanted to back out of the trip a dozen times, but under the threat of annihilation from his mother, he decided to go. My country boy had been "coughing up a lung," as he likes to say, for weeks. His mother was going to take him to a specialist, so the trip to Dawsonville was perfect timing. He spoke with such a pronounced Georgia accent that he almost needed an interpreter to understand what he said. What he said this time, however, didn't need any interpretation. Suddenly, as a giant light bulb when off in his head, what he blurted was music to my ears, "I ain't been coughin'!" "Of course, you haven't," I returned with a smile and wink, looking at him in my rearview mirror.

On another occasion, I took a student that I knew had a prophetic call on his life. He had lived through crazy family chaos and lots of pain growing up. He endured being shuffled around while his parents were incarcerated back-to-back as a result of a scandalous tragedy that framed them both for a crime they didn't commit. I knew his story and had prophesied into his calling. But Marty, the pastor in the water, didn't know the backstory.

My jaw dropped at Marty's first statement, "You have never felt wanted or loved in your family, and Jesus wants to touch that part of you." (It wasn't that he wasn't wanted or loved, but that's the lie the enemy sold him because of what happened to his family, and it had penetrated his heart.) Visibly, the shame of feeling unwanted reddened his face and brought tears to his eyes. In a holy moment of Holy Spirit access, he came fully present to the depth of hurt and pain that had up to this point been irretrievably locked in the recesses of his soul. Coming up out of the water, he radiated and was overwhelmed with joy. Now, no longer captive to his past, Marty blew his world up in the best way, prophesying that he was indeed a prophet called to the nations.

These four boys epitomize what God is doing in erasing a lifetime of shame in ONE ENCOUNTER. The power of the baptism revival is that those who have been drawn to the waters have come with their hands open and their hearts primed for transformation. Having been prepared ahead of time by the Holy Spirit for this hallmark moment in their lives, the desperate and hungry come with no other agenda than to have their hearts made right, aligned with Heaven, and free from every encumbrance that has thwarted their efforts to know the God of Fire intimately. As the Fire of God descends upon them in the waters of baptism, suddenly Grace on steroids is tangibly present to break into long-fortified walls of self-protection. The orphan entombed within those walls comes to life, leaving the filthy rags of their shame and sin at the bottom of the pool.

These boys' stories paint the picture of salvation and transformation in this era of great acceleration. Jesus is doing in a holy moment what has taken many of us years to see happen in our lives. His process for healing the masses is evolving and birthing a radical restoration of the "Gadarene Demoniac Generation" (Mark 5). Like the Gadarene who was released from "Legion," an angry mob of demons, many in this generation will be healed in ONE MOMENT, and out of that encounter, they will be launched into their destinies. They will bypass the formal and religious systems of learning and preach the Kingdom, telling everyone they meet what Jesus did for them. This power is available to YOU.

Pray this with me:

Jesus, I look to You alone as the One who heals me and takes away my shame. Your still small Voice is as big to me as Your Voice thundering in the mountains. As I navigate the world's chaos, Your Voice tethers me to the reality of the Unseen Real. What I cannot see is more real than what I am looking at right now. Father, I know perception is everything. Heal my myopic vision and bring the revelation that opens the eyes of my heart to the reality of who You are. I seek Your face, not what You're holding in Your hands. I declare that You are a good, good Father and that I am not moved by what my circumstances dictate. I am moved by Your Spirit and every breath You breathe. I declare that I do not have to understand everything to trust the One who crafted me in His image and whose very breath gives me life. I say, "Come, Holy Spirit and encounter me in such a way that, like the Gadarene demoniac, I am transformed in a moment to never again be the same."

DAY 20

Orphan Dream

"I will not leave you as orphans; I will come to you."

-*NIV*, JOHN 14:18

"But You have seen, for You observe trouble and grief, to repay it by Your hand. The helpless commits himself to You; You are the helper of the fatherless."

-*NIV*, PSALM 10:14

I had a dream several years ago about an orphan that had been living in my house for years—without me even knowing it. In the dream, this child was about two or three feet tall, and he was greasy, dirty, totally unkempt, and looked like he was homeless. He was reminiscent of Tarzan because he looked like a child raised in the wild, lacking social skills and unaccustomed to human contact or interaction. In the dream, we walked up and down the mall looking for a place that sold ice cream, and even though it existed, we could never actually find it. At one point, in my exasperation in the hunt for ice cream, I noticed that this kid was eating what looked like the thrown-away remains of a dirty, melted, chocolate-covered ice cream bar that someone had decided they were finished with and thrown in the trash. I was repulsed by this child's crude manner of enjoying someone else's garbage.

As I led him by the hand, I kept thinking I needed to take this kid home and get him in the shower as soon as possible. I wanted to clean him up fast. In the way that you know things in dreams that you wouldn't know in real life, I was suddenly aware that this child would not only not want a bath, but that he had been living in my house for years without me knowing he existed.

He had lived in the recesses and hidden places in the house, escaping notice as he consumed the garbage, leftovers, and anything else he could scrounge. I am generally a loving person and love children and young adults with ease, but in the dream, I was alienated from this kid in a way that didn't call forth a normal loving response in my heart. Yet I knew that he was not used to love or human touch. At one point, knowing how uncivilized he was, I thought, "I need to shake him up with some harsh discipline and whip him into shape." Essentially, I needed to assert my authority and tell this kid to get it together and fly right—yet I knew his alienation and unfamiliarity with human interaction would preclude any response to a demand on my part.

As I was pacing the floor, recounting this part of the dream to my wife, it dawned on me that the orphaned boy was me. He was a part of me that I was estranged from. During the timeframe of this dream, my wife and I had been doing a Daniel fast, basically being vegans for 21 days in response to a call for a fast from our pastor. I had done a Daniel fast several times before and found it refreshing and cleansing. But this time, my attitude was not so good.

I found myself irritated and angry at times, partially because my wife and I had been doing an anti-cancer diet since the time my wife was diagnosed with stage-three breast (she was miraculously healed but continued the diet). I am the cook in our house, and we were on a gluten-free, everything-free, no-fun-at-all, diet already in which I felt utterly lost as a cook. How many ways can you cook cauliflower? I had already roasted it, mashed, steamed, whatever-elsed it! I was annoyed that I had to give up chicken and fish, too. I was annoyed because nothing tasted good to me, and an apple for dessert just made me want to curse and have a big, fat tantrum. When my wife just mentioned giving up coffee on her diet in the car, I blurted, "Don't even talk to me about giving up Starbucks because I'm not! I am going to keep one thing that I flipping enjoy on the table!" I dug my heels deep in humorous protest, but there was less humor in it than I feigned.

More than irritation, what I had been feeling for several days on this fast was like I wanted to fall in a heap on the floor and cry. Every day, I was on the verge of having an emotional breakdown. One TV series that we like to watch in the evening is "Heartland," a show highlighting a family who own and run a cattle and horse ranch in a small town in Alberta, Canada. The stories are about how a family interacts with each other in the midst of conflict. It's messy, but they love each other and ultimately make the right decisions with integrity and love. It may be a bit cheesy for some, but it was now making me tear up several times during the show.

Something was popping up in my heart, and I could not tuck it away. I had been irritable and emotional for days, and the dream shed light on what was happening to me. All I had to do was pull back another layer of creature comfort, my food addiction, and suddenly I was forced to come present to my heart—a part of my heart that I had been able to keep at bay through my addiction to food and filling the empty places in the day with entertainment and distraction.

For years, I had had deep loneliness in my heart that no human interaction could touch. My birth was premature. I was four pounds and born two months early. Back in the day, babies were in incubators when born premature, and I was in one for six weeks. Incubators at that time were not interactive like they are today. I probably went for most hours of every day without being touched. I have jokingly always said, "I think I bonded with the emptiness," and laughed it off, knowing that there was some truth to what I was saying (I don't say it anymore after my wife said one day that there was nothing remotely funny about it and that I was bonded to Jesus now). Given the painful aloneness I had felt through the years, it made sense. Now, on a Daniel fast, I was coming present to my own heart in a way that Jesus could access and be present with me.

Jesus, in the absence of my numbing agents and addictions, was showing me the orphan in my own heart—an orphan that I needed to make peace with and heal. The orphan's name is "Shame." Until we can embrace the orphaned places within us and bless the longings of the orphan that lead us into addiction, we will never break the power that shame wields in our hearts and minds.

Shame is the foundation that every addiction is built upon. The enemy's biggest weapon propagated against a generation of orphaned children is to perpetuate the lie that we are alienated from His love and that we must "give the orphan a shower" to make ourselves acceptable. The enemy does not waste any opportunity to fuel the lies that our shame, unchecked by Truth, compels us to believe.

Counter to shame's accusation that we are defective beyond measure—irreparably damaged goods, fit only for the trash heap—is the Truth that we are fully loved in whatever condition we are in. Jesus is not caught off guard with our humanity. He is not offended by our struggle and descent into hellish addictions used to numb the pain of our orphaned hearts. In order to bless our story, including the dark parts that we have the hardest time forgiving, we must relinquish our hold on shame and the lies that have kept us embroiled in the struggle. Jesus' burning passion is to rescue the orphan, the widow, the harassed, the bruised, oppressed, unwanted, and the unloved. In His Presence, all things "become," and the orphan in the man or woman finds a home. Paul, a saint much acquainted with both the orphan named "Shame" and the sonship of our Heavenly Father, admonishes us that, "The Spirit you received does not make you slaves so that you live in fear again; rather, the Spirit you received brought about your adoption to sonship. And by him, we cry, "Abba, Father" (*NIV*, Rom. 8:15).

Pray this with me:

Jesus, I thank You that the orphan—the lost, unloved part of me—finds a home in You. Father, pour out your Spirit of adoption on me and gather every part of me that I have been alienated or estranged from. Rescue any and every part of me that Your Love has not apprehended. Leave the ninety-nine, Lord Jesus, and come after me, the "one," and never allow me to wander from Your grasp. Jesus, be larger than every addiction that I have ever engaged with, that I would be won by your Kindness that leads me to repentance, the place of changing my mind and changing how I see You—changing how I see and know who I am in You. Lord, Your Kindness transforms the orphan into a love child—a child who knows love well and can extend that love in the places where I am still tempted to keep myself "on the hook." Lord, I declare that as You dismantle shame in my life, I am becoming even more deeply acquainted with Your love. Your love conquers all fear and makes me bold, tells me who I am, and empowers me to re-present You to a world that is desperate to know what Love looks like. In Jesus' Name, Amen.

DAY 21

Shame and the Law

"Woe to you, teachers of the law and Pharisees, you hypocrites! You clean the outside of the cup and dish, but inside they are full of greed and self-indulgence. Blind Pharisee! First clean the inside of the cup and dish, and then the outside also will be clean."

-*NIV*, MATT. 23:25-26

Holiness birthed from a transformational, ongoing encounter with the Holy Spirit produces the fruit of intimacy and purity of heart. External holiness, whether as a covert mandate or as something well-articulated from the platform, masquerades as the pathway to righteousness. But at its core is demonically infused legalism that preys on our shame and propensity to find life in "getting it right" or fulfilling the law. But in the flames of revival, when raw, unfettered love and kindness lead us to repentance, our perspectives are completely reoriented in ways that only our newly awakened heart to Love could conceive.

I remember going to local churches during a season that I was doing conferences and seminars on healing from past abuse of every kind. We would invite Holy Spirit to come into the places of wounding and heal the addictions that came as a result of people attempting to fill the gaping holes in their souls.

I went to a couple of "holiness" churches and spoke to

pastors about the possibility of doing one of my conferences in their churches. I was unanimously met with, "We don't have those kinds of problems in our church," and would be dismissed by a pastor shaking his head at my audacity to suggest such things. I have heard countless stories of many churches who preach "holiness at all costs" on the outside but are a carnival of adultery and fornication on the inside. I sat in a youth meeting for one of these very holy churches. I almost came utterly unhinged when I heard the youth pastor's parting admonition to a room full of teenagers, "Okay boys, no playing with your joysticks this week and no playing with your lily pads, girls!" I almost threw up on the spot, but I wasn't sure what penance for a dirty carpet would look like for me. I am sure that all those teenagers promptly refrained. I'm not making a judgment—the Pharisee and sinner both find redemption at the foot of the Cross. I am just creating a picture of what false holiness often looks like.

One of Jesus' most incredible accusations levied against the Pharisees was their gatekeeping—their determination of who gets in the club and who gets hurled out the door on their head. Their shame was seen in their arrogance, pride, and gross assumption that the outside of the cup mattered the most. Jesus drew a pointed contrast to His thinking and theirs, "But the things that come out of a person's mouth come from the heart, and these defile them" (*NIV*, Matt. 15:18). The outside of the cup too often is the primary measure we use to evaluate a person's spiritual condition. It is easy to clean the outside of the cup by conformity to the rules. If we are good, we can all get our checkboxes checked and maybe get a gold star at the end.

There are multiple problems with this, but here's the main problem—conformity to the law produces compliance at best, but it will never call forth love and passion. The standard of the law propels us into sin and plays well in our shame – the shame we experience every time we fail. Shame and law are inexorably intertwined, and the devil himself fortifies their marriage. Why? Religion is impotent. A church full of religious "Christians" is the enemy's dream; therefore, his investment in provoking our shame, causing us to feel separated, alone, condemned, and disconnected, is enormous. Shame is at the core of all evil, and provoking our shame is the enemy's favorite weapon.

The law can only produce fear and shame in our failure to keep it. Only love, devoid of fear, can coax open a heart shut down in fear. Love is the Grand Motivator of the Holy Spirit that calls us into a place of surrender where we can feel protected and safe in our vulnerability. The One that beckons us to come will not hurt us and is not playing a game of hide and seek – hiding when we have not jumped through the hoop or missed the mark. Jesus is not afraid of the mess – He entered the mess and redeemed it. He is not afraid of our humanity and is not caught off guard or surprised by our darkest moments.

The biggest challenge for most of us is in accessing His forgiveness and letting ourselves off the hook. If shame could have its way with us, it would keep us perpetually tethered to condemnation and the unshakable feeling that we are irrevocably flawed, defective, and deserving of death. But the Pharisees then and now have gotten it all wrong.

The good news is that this burden of guilt and condemnation doesn't win – not when we take the greatest leap of faith ever and choose to say "yes" to the One who paid in His own Blood for our freedom – all for the sake of love. He alone offers us an unfathomable, reason-defying, never gonna wrap our head around it, ain't no way to earn it, never gonna make sense of it, just need to accept it – gift. One "yes" and the house of cards the devil builds with our shame comes crashing down with no hope of reprisal. Jesus wins.

Pray this with me:

Jesus, I will never be able to wrap my head around Your sacrifice that made me righteous in Your eyes for all eternity. The concept of a free gift, a transfer of righteousness from Your account to mine by an act of faith, is mind-blowing. I can make a daily choice to trust You and, by that choice, shame's hold on me is broken and rendered null and void. The illusion of separation was blown to smithereens at the Cross, and I do not have to do anything to earn Your love or Your sacrifice. ALL THIS goes against everything in my natural mind and screams "Wrong, wrong, wrong!!" It is so far beyond my wildest imagination that I don't know what to do with myself when I ponder it but a minute. Yet the truth is that You are Right, right, right! So I just say, "Yes," and I tell my thoughts to shut up because my heart receives it. After all, I was made for love. For YOUR love. Thank You, Jesus. Thank You, thank You, with all my heart I thank You. Amen.

DAY 22

Destiny Destroys Shame

When Esther's words were reported to Mordecai, he sent back this answer: "Do not think that because you are in the king's house, you alone of all the Jews will escape. For if you remain silent at this time, relief and deliverance for the Jews will arise from another place, but you and your father's family will perish. And who knows but that you have come to your royal position for such a time as this?"

-*NIV*, ESTHER 4:12-14

There is an inherent sense of shame, whether we are aware enough to label it or not, embedded in our disconnection to purpose and destiny. As Image bearers, we cannot discover who we are apart from the One who created us. He alone owns the right to define us as His creation. Many of the wounds that this generation, together with older generations, carry in their souls are the byproduct of a fractured culture and family unit. They have left us with gaping, bloody holes in our souls due to rejection, abandonment, abuse of every variety, and deprivation. We are like heat-seeking missiles, looking for an unsuspecting target so we can get our needs met and fill the hollow places inside.

The longing, itself, is good—it is the very thing that draws us to seek out the One who made us for wholeness. Things go awry when our needs and longings drive us to meet them apart from, and in ways that separate us from. the Creator. Our propensity to find meaning, identity and approval from the created rather than the Creator compounds and perpetuates our shame while forestalling the destiny that Heaven has carved out for us before we existed on earth.

Partnering with Heaven and connecting with what we were made for calls us up and out of our need for the creature to tell us who we are and chart our life course.

Esther did not know that she held a trump card in the grand scheme of Heaven to save the Jews from Haman's evil plan for destruction. Everything in her life up to this point was preparation for this moment. Esther experienced Heavenly convergence where preparation meets divine appointment and favor. Like many of us, Esther did not have a destiny map that enabled her to see exactly what she was being prepared for, but she was faithful to do the next thing — to show up in the places she knew she needed to — and favor did the rest. Mordecai was the agent God used to call her forth prophetically into the most significant chapter in her Book of Life (Psalm 139). This is what she was made for, and when she responded in a way that honored God, the Jews who were scheduled for destruction through royal decree — including Esther and Mordecai — were delivered.

It has always struck me that she was invited with a caveat. The caveat in verse 14 is that if she had chosen silence, God had a backup plan — He would bring deliverance from another place. One cannot miss the clarion call that God gives us in the words of Mordecai to Esther, "For if you remain silent at this time, relief and deliverance for the Jews will arise from another place, but you and your father's family will perish ..."

God, in His love, mercy and great passion, launched us

into the greater works and exploits crafted by Heaven specifically for us "…for such a time as this." Most of the students I work with in my regular English classes are rough around the edges. Many have experienced more trauma in their short lives than many adults that I know. It ranges from having incarcerated parents, drug abuse and/or physical abuse in the home, having a child of their own, not living in the same home with the same relative consistently, coming to school always hungry, lacking medical care, having tumultuous relationships, and more—all of which lead to feelings of despair and hopelessness. They are toxically shamed and lack the infrastructure and scaffolding for growth that would set them up for success. They epitomize the kind of crowds that Jesus felt deep compassion for because they were "…harassed and helpless, like sheep without a shepherd" (*NIV*, Matt. 9:36).

Shame is this generation's most formidable enemy. It keeps them tethered to a life familiar with shattered dreams and great uncertainty and anxiety about the future because their experiences have told them that they are defective, not enough, and that dreams are not for people like them.

As a teacher, my most significant responsibility is not teaching the content of my course but instilling hope, purpose, and destiny in my students. (Okay, before you hang me out to dry as a bad teacher, what good is teaching the content if they can't actually do anything with it? They need to feel loved and have a sense of value for anything else to matter. I am, however, not undermining the importance of education and the need for teaching good curriculum.)

For many, their educational experiences parallel their life experiences, leaving them devoid of confidence in the goodness of the world. The harvest is ripe, and it is profoundly apparent that God's heart is to invade a generation that is poised for launch at the precipice of the greatest revival the world has ever known. Thankfully, "...God chose the foolish things of the world to shame the wise; God chose the weak things of the world to shame the strong" (*NIV*, 1 Cor. 1:27).

Connecting a generation to the future ordained by God and written in the Book of their lives is the biggest shame-buster ever. Shame disconnects and separates and can only promote a hopeless, meaningless life. Love never fails, and as the Lover of our souls, He longs to collaborate with us and with the heart of this generation. As mothers and fathers, we are to be the conduit of Heaven's investment in this generation, and the currency we've been given to invest in them is our time, our love and words of life and destiny. Spending it well is to prophetically call forth the manifest sons and daughters of God.

As Image bearers, we find our identity, promised future, and destiny in our union with Jesus. In a generation that is steeped in toxic shame, they must not only believe in the Resurrected One who wrote the Book of Life, but they must also encounter Him. In encountering the Holy Spirit, we can be awakened to our true selves. Once awakened, we are ushered into our predestined journey, established before we were ever conceived. In His Presence, we "become" all things and find our way in the adventure we were created to live. The power of shame will disintegrate as you continue to encounter His presence and prophetically connect to the purpose, calling, gifting, and mission that is bound in the Book of Life — the one with your name inscribed on it.

Pray this with me:

Jesus, I choose You. I ask that You reveal to me a piece of my destiny that You conceived before I was ever conceived here on earth. Father, I look to You to tell me who I am and why You created me and put me on this planet. My purpose, life, and all the exploits as a manifest son or daughter are found in You alone. Encounter me in a way that opens the eyes and ears of my heart and my spirit so that encountering You becomes my new normal. I want everything You have for me. I lay my plan at Your feet and take up Yours — in Jesus' Name. Amen.

DAY 23

Freedom from the Voice of Saul

"Then I will give you shepherds after My own heart, who will lead you with knowledge and understanding."

-NIV, JER. 3:15

Saul is an enigmatic character in the Old Testament. Protagonists in the stories we love to read evolve and grow, becoming wiser and more self-aware as the story unfolds. There is always a decisive moment when they must make a choice to either lay their own lives down or save themselves. Heroes, in this sense, are more made than born as their characters are refined in the cauldron of trials, tests, and seemingly insurmountable challenges. Saul's story starts with a bang, but what had the potential to be an inspiring rags-to-riches story ends very badly as the drama becomes a tragedy. Saul becomes an antagonist to the Almighty God and a gross disappointment to the prophet who anointed him king. His insecurity is his fatal flaw—one that echoes in the prophet Samuel's lament, "When you were small in your own sight, were you not made the head of the tribes of Israel, and the Lord anointed you king over Israel?... Why then did you not obey the voice of the Lord but swooped down upon the plunder and did evil in the Lord's sight? (*NIV*, 1 Sam. 15:17,19). (To get the full story of Saul, read 1 Sam. 9-31).

Saul's narcissistic insecurity found its greatest expression when under pressure, like many leaders today.

Under pressure, Saul raged when he was thwarted in his endeavors to affirm his kingship, and he sought to annihilate anyone who threatened his authority. His rage and irrational attacks on David were fueled by his self-protective commitment to avoid rejection at all costs. He felt exposed and grossly overshadowed by David's gifting, success, and favor with God and man. Yet David refused to take retribution for this injustice into his own hands.

The voice of Saul that we hear in our heads is the voice of every leader who hurt us to elevate themselves while relegating us to a lesser place. Lacking in true redemptive self-awareness, Sauls use their position to forward their agendas, consequently running roughshod over those who carry a different spirit. Functioning from a fractured soul, riddled by deep insecurities and fear of rejection, they are incapable of functioning as true fathers or mothers in the faith whose core motivation is to serve and empower those around them—pushing them forward regardless of how far they surpass them (however, through repentance and a revelation of the grace and love of God, a Saul can be transformed into a David). Fathers are not threatened by those who are more gifted, powerful, or have more favor and influence than they do. They are servants first, and they leverage their influence through relationship to bless and launch their spiritual sons and daughters into their promised futures. More on that in a minute.

Many years ago, I had a stirring in my heart to start a non-profit ministry that would come outside of the traditional church and minister to the ones that the church had discarded—particularly those who were sexually addicted. Many sincere Christians refuse to walk into a church and talk about the darkest aspects of life and struggle because they were kicked out or walked out with their heads heavy upon their chests in shame. The church might be able to handle alcoholism, divorce recovery (depending on the circumstances), and other not-so-dirty or only semi-messy issues if they have a program to shuffle them into. But there are many wounded and broken people the church has either been unwilling to or didn't have the power to help or to set free.

As I launched this entrepreneurial ministry venture, I was railroaded by an emergency meeting at the request of my pastor and a few elders, who promptly brought me in for a sit-down. They opened the meeting with prayer, and then read the following scripture to me: "Whoever remains stiff-necked after many rebukes will suddenly be destroyed — without remedy" (*NIV*, Prov. 29:1).

That meeting devastated me beyond belief. Basically, what I was being told is that if I went forward with a ministry that was not under my current church as an arm of that church (and they were not offering for it to be), I would be under a curse. My character, walk with Jesus, and response to authority structures were all called into question because I wanted to do something in a way that they didn't approve of. They viewed para-church ministry as unscriptural. According to them, everything needed to come under the umbrella — and control — of church leadership. I'm not anti-church by any means, but the church structure has often reflected the world system, just like the religious system did in Jesus' day. It is too often geared around the desire for power, control, and money, and inadvertently becomes its own political system.

These church leaders used "spiritual covering" as a weapon to cut me open emotionally and spiritually. Don't get me wrong — I'm not saying they shouldn't have had input. As leaders of the church I attended, their opinions carried weight and there are issues they may have seen that it would've been appropriate for them to speak into. But there is a vast difference between loving input and spiritual cursing.

There are differing views on spiritual covering, but the best and healthiest way I've heard it described is that we cover with love those we hold in our hearts. So, you have spiritual authority in the lives of those you love and honor, in the safety of relationship. It's not authority to direct their lives. It's power to bless and to give life to another. There is room for corrective words in that context, in a relationship of love. Anything else leads to exploitation and various forms of spiritual abuse.

Essentially, what my leaders did was curse me. I don't remember what I said in that meeting. I only remember the deep confusion, hurt, and shock I left with. And shame. Somewhere after the first two minutes, my head disconnected as it all became surreal. I was told that I would be broken beyond compare if I left the "covering" of their church. In any other realm of life, we would call what happened a form of bullying and emotional abuse.

For me, it was simple. I wanted to help the disenfranchised, broken, and wounded — the ones the church discarded. The passion I had for the mission God put in my heart had almost been obliterated that day — but the Holy Spirit blew on the smoldering wick and healed the bruised reed. The ministry got up and running and served hundreds of people who needed to know what an encounter with the Truth could do in a life ravaged by sin and struggle. "A bruised reed he will not break, and a smoldering wick he will not snuff out till he has brought justice through to victory" (*NIV*, Matt. 12:20).

So back to the concept of "covering." In many churches, under the guise of submission to spiritual authority, it functions as a control method. We saw the most significant illustration of this dysfunction in the Shepherding Movement of the 1980s.

Personal accountability should not occur in the context of a leader's positional authority. Everyone wants a title so they can wield authority over someone else. The leader who leads from a place of positional power will only call forth compliance out of fear—devoid of passion and love. The ones who motivate people to pursue God with passion and to listen to what Holy Spirit is saying to them, and who empower them to do what they are gifted and designed to do (in other words, the ones who serve)—these are the true leaders.

We acknowledge and submit to positional authority, particularly in the context of the workplace, where hierarchical structures still exist. The boss has the power to hire and fire, to promote or demote, and our paychecks are on the line. However, personal accountability for the believer is meant to take place in the context of RELATIONSHIP as an organic function of the Body of Christ.

Accountability happens naturally with those we trust and feel safe with. So, we submit as an act of volition—not under compulsion or fear of retribution. We also have the power to disagree. It is not a dictatorship. Loving correction is not a scary thing in the context of relationship, and it frees us to grow and mature.

Many leaders, in their insecurity and brokenness, use their position to enforce personal accountability, which is tantamount to a form of "holy" slavery. We must never coerce someone to bend to our will. This is manipulation and is a form of witchcraft. I will follow any leader who is both transparent and a servant.

Servant leaders lead from the bottom up—empowering those they serve—beckoning them to establish their footing at the highest point of their anointing, impact, and journey with Jesus. They lay down their lives for the generation they seek to launch, allowing them to build on their backs, so to speak. Servant leaders call forth the gold in those they serve and seek every opportunity to launch them into their destiny. Servant leaders, like good parents, want to see those in whom they are investing their lives surpass them—taking the torch of the Kingdom of God and blazing uncharted territory both in ministry and in the Spirit.

Pray this with me:

Lord, teach me to be a good learner, one who yields to others, and one who leads like Jesus did — as a servant. Once again, I open my hand to You, Jesus, and give You the ones that I have been privileged to serve, empower, exhort, and launch that they might destroy the kingdom of darkness. I thank You for the role that You have given me to come alongside Your DREAD CHAMPIONS and MANIFEST SONS and DAUGHTERS OF GOD. Father, give me wisdom from Heaven, anointing without measure, and the courage to always seek to serve first and bless ALL that You are doing in the Generation. I say, "send me," commission me and demonstrate Your power and love through me, as one You can trust to further Your Kingdom and do Your will — on Earth as it is in Heaven. In Your Son's Name. Amen.

DAY 24

Positioned in Unshakable Grace

"When Jesus was tortured and then crucified on the cross, He performed a violent act of grace. The cross became a battering ram that smashed through the iron bars of the Law...allowing the unworthy (that would be us) into the Kingdom of God...Jesus was crucified as us, not just for us, and His righteousness became ours."

-KRIS VALLOTTON[18]

The healing para-church ministry that I mentioned in the previous chapter primarily ministered to the most addicted and broken in our culture. And I knew something about that from personal experience. The gatherings at my conferences and intensive multi-week recovery groups looked a lot like the crowds that Jesus hung out with.

One of my many favorite scenes in the TV series, "The Chosen,"[19] which depicts the most tangible, human Jesus I have ever encountered on the screen, is when a crowd has gathered outside of the home of His disciples, James and John, the sons

---

[18] Vallotton, K. (2015). School of the prophets: Advanced training for prophetic ministry. Minneapolis, MN: Chosen.

[19] Jenkins, D. (2017-). The Chosen [Television series]. USA: VidAngel Studios.

of Zebedee. The Romans and Pharisees alike suddenly materialize outside the windows of the house, which is chock-full of some of the most unsavory characters of the day.

The sounds of the roof being wedged apart interrupt Jesus' teaching as the desperate friends of a paralytic man lower their white-knuckled friend, hands wrapped tightly around the rope, to the feet of Jesus. Ignoring the bloviating Pharisees, indignant at the window, He turns his sights first to the pleading eyes of faith above him and then to the determined eyes of the paralytic and says, "Son, your sins are forgiven." Then, after letting the Pharisees know He could hear them screaming "blasphemer" in their heads, He boldly affirms His authority as the Son of Man to both forgive sins and heal the sick.

The Pharisees today are equally offended with the extravagant grace of a Savior who isn't afraid of the mess in our lives—who enters into the mess and locks eyes with us in the midst of our most unseemly moments of shame. While we're feeling utterly bankrupt, He assures us that we are passionately loved and never forsaken in our failures and mistakes.

A great tragedy in our generation is that so many of the broken and wounded have experienced so much hurt by the Church's inability to respond to people whose mess falls outside parameters of their conditional grace. Grace in the church today is often hypocritically based upon one's ability to clean up and get it right, turning it into works and not grace after all. This form of "grace" aborts the very process of sanctification that Jesus seeks to usher us into.

Just like Adam in the Garden abdicated his innocence and righteousness through an ongoing relationship with God and chose a pursuit of the knowledge of good and evil through his own efforts, the Israelites in the desert were content with

Moses and the Law rather than God Himself. At fallen man's core is a hardened, sinful desire to establish righteousness through self-effort. Until we surrender our attempts to manage our lives, we will remain tethered to the Law and fail to apprehend the true freedom that only the Blood of Jesus has appropriated for us. We will continue to be captives relegated to the hell of self.

The people that came into the ministry that I did during that season struggled with every kind of sexual addiction and had painful pasts of abuse and trauma. Every week they came shrouded in the shame of that week's failures and attempts to do the right thing. They loved Jesus and were inexorably drawn to His promise of mercy, grace, and restoration for their damaged souls. The deep-seated sense of failure compounded their shame as a Christian. They struggled to reconcile their love and passion for God and the struggle that seemed to dominate their lives and sabotaged every effort they made to live a holy life.

The premise that undergirded their shame was the lie that their failure separated them from God. In their woundedness, they projected onto God the dysfunctional belief about who He was as a father. The unwritten rules and ways of perceiving who they were as the product of their upbringing became the unhealthy lens through which they viewed God.

The enemy seeks to gain significant ground in the heart of the believer by propagating the lie that they are separated from God, much like the child who, after a blow-up with a parent, retreats into the background waiting for the moment when the mood of the parent feels safe enough to emerge again to reestablish a connection.

In safe environments and relationships with other Believers, this kind of toxic belief can be viewed in proper perspective. Because the context of our wounding is the family of origin, the healing of our personhood must also be healed in "family" as we mediate the Presence of Jesus. In His Presence, we become...everything. As God places us into a family of Believers who are Presence-oriented and seek to facilitate and host the habitation of His Presence, we meet Jesus in our place of need. He heals, renames, and assures us that we are never separated from Him.

Our worst and best moments are met with the same fierce love of a Father who seeks to reconcile us to Him, others, and to the parts of us that we have become estranged from in our attempts to meet legitimate needs for love, acceptance, and affirmation apart from the One who created us. In this way, He heals our faulty perceptions and assures us that our position in Him is never compromised.

When we see Him rightly and we see ourselves in relation to Him rightly, we also see that our engagement in the sin struggles themselves cannot separate us from Him. We are one with Him, and our Oneness with Him started the minute we were born again. Our perception of separation from Him when our sense shame is the most poignant is merely a smokescreen of the enemy designed to perpetuate the cycle of shame.

Suppose we step out of our immovable position in Christ Jesus (where we are always righteous, always holy, always loved), which can only happen in our perception, and engage with the accusation and lie of the enemy in our struggle that God has turned away from us. At that point, we must decide how long we want to hang out in the enemy's delusion. Do we want to hang in the lie for 10 minutes, a day, a month, five years? Or do we cast down the imaginations of the enemy, and realign ourselves with the truth of our ever-only righteous standing before God (because Christ died for us, as us) immediately?

The world system's lie is that every failure sends us back to ground zero. In the Kingdom of God's economy, we go from "glory to glory." We are not the same person today, even in our struggle, as we were when we were unreconciled to God. We never go backwards in the Kingdom—we never go back to square one. The beauty of Jesus' finished work on the Cross is that it IS finished, and we must let go of our attempt to crucify Him afresh or crucify ourselves through self-contempt.

If we stay in the lie and accusation of the enemy, we must ask ourselves this question, "What investment do I have in punishing myself when God is not?" To live victoriously, we must change our language and perceptions. We must "repent" and see rightly who we are as ones who are in a union with Christ that can never be broken or misaligned. We must choose to renounce the lie of separation, affirm our righteousness as the Gift of Christ, and determine to close the illusory gap that we feel when the enemy assaults our right-standing with God. Even in the midst of struggles that only God can deliver us from, our faith is in the God who never changes, who is always in a good mood, and who locks eyes with me and never averts His gaze.

Am I saying here that it is okay to hang out in sin and bondage? What I'm saying is that the way out is through relationship, through staying engaged with God and listening for His affirming voice, allowing Him to heal our hearts. He longs to set us free. But contrary to the voice of the Father, all the voice of shame does is to wrap us even more tightly to sin, bondage and addiction. It has no power to deliver. The grace that God extends is infused with the power to set me free. It gives me the power to repent, to change my mind, to align myself with His thoughts about me. It keeps me connected to the Source, and that is where true freedom is found.

Pray this with me:

Jesus, we thank You that You bring healing and love into our lives in many forms—through mothers and fathers in the faith, children (spiritual and natural-born), grandchildren, other family members, friends, community, and more. We thank You that Your promises fulfilled are a tree a life to us, nurturing our hearts. As You reveal Your faithfulness to us and show us who You are—such a good, good, Father—the shame that has been so toxic in our hearts and that compelled us to believe so many lies about ourselves, others, and even You, just melts away. Your goodness melts our hearts and removes our shame, and You, oh Lord, only You, call us to stand upright in You where we find our true selves! I declare that I have many spiritual sons and daughters. My spiritual and natural-born children will love God passionately and serve Him with their whole hearts. They will fulfill their destinies in the Kingdom and do great exploits in His Name.

DAY 25

Prayer for Breaking Trauma Over Our Bodies and Releasing Resurrection

I will restore to you the years that the swarming locust has eaten, the hopper, the destroyer, and the cutter, my great army, which I sent among you.

-ESV, JOEL 2:25

For you created my inmost being;
you knit me together in my mother's womb.
I praise you because I am fearfully and
wonderfully made;
your works are wonderful, I know that full well.
My frame was not hidden from you when I was
made in the secret place, when I was woven
together in the depths of the earth.
Your eyes saw my unformed body;
all the days ordained for me were written in your
book before one of them came to be.

-NIV, PS. 139:13-16

As creatures who are spirit, soul, and body intertwined into one, made in the image of God, we cannot be neatly broken down into parts. One cannot say that my body experienced this trauma, but my emotions were not touched. Paul gives us a clue from another angle regarding sexual immorality, "Do you not know that he who unites himself with a prostitute is one with her body? For it is said, 'The two will become one flesh.' But whoever is united with the Lord is one with him in spirit." Not only do we trade DNA with the one we join ourselves to sexually, but every part of our being is also engaged. This union of spirit, soul, and body gives trauma much power to damage us. Trauma introduced early in life is like scrambling the inside of the unborn chick in the shell. If the raw, unformed substance of a chicken is traumatized before it becomes a fully developed little chick, it will fail to thrive and die. Similarly, early trauma can be the most damaging because its impact is pervasive to every part of the child.

The good news is that there is not anything that the Cross cannot undo. All things are reversible in Jesus. The process of undoing what has been done to us that caused significant trauma is not always tit-for-tat or an equal measure of one thing for another. Heaven's repayment plan, what God does when He restores what has been stolen, lost, or destroyed in our lives, is exponential—it is exceedingly, abundantly, beyond, whatever we can imagine.

Restoration may not look exactly like we expect but the depth and breadth of what God does will astound us. He often compacts so much into a moment of our lives that we can hardly believe it as He reconciles the broken places and heals our broken hearts. These are the good 'suddenlies' of life that can wipe away years of trauma.

I remember a discussion in one of my clinical counseling classes many years ago about the impact of sexual abuse. Some students wanted to add weight to different kinds of sexual abuse like fondling, sexual penetration, voyeurism, and rough sexual language. The problem in looking at sexual abuse through that lens is that perception is everything, and trauma is not measured by the deed but by its impact on the human heart, the mind and the body. For example, a child being fondled can be as traumatizing in its effect on the individual's soul as being penetrated sexually or being raped.

A key to ministering to someone who has experienced trauma is knowing that the healing of one part, like their memories or emotional damage, does not always translate into healing for the other parts of their being, like their bodies. As intertwined beings, the healing of one part of us can undoubtedly impact and free up the other parts of our being. Still, some parts may require greater attention somewhere in the process that enables us to fully integrate healing throughout our being. The body remembers and stores the trauma in its very cells. Releasing the body from injury and making decrees and declarations over our body can catapult us into a place of more impacting healing that changes how we think, act, and feel about ourselves. The shame that has held us gets busted in the chops when broken off our bodies.

Because it's the truth that sets us free, we will focus on speaking words of truth over ourselves. The Holy Spirit is the One who washes us clean, and He uses our own words in conjunction with His to do it. Therefore, the focus of this devotional is the prayer. Pray the following prayer slowly, being sure to linger in every place that He leads, enabling the Holy Spirit to speak specifically into areas that may need to be prayed for or blessed.

Pray this with me:

Jesus, I start with my head, and I break the power of the spirit of trauma over my head. I ask that You wash over my mind—healing everything that impacted my brain in any adverse way, and anything that negatively affected the way I think. Pour your oil through every synapse and open every place that has ever been shut down or stunted—from birth throughout life. Jesus, you know all that my eyes have seen— the things that I know about and those that I don't even remember. Wash through my memories—everything that I have taken in, that I participated in and those that were forced upon me. Wash away the trauma, shock, and everything that sexualized me too early, that put things into my sight before I was emotionally, mentally, and spiritually ready to see and process.

Father, everything that I participated in too soon brought me into an adult world when I was so impressionable. I am asking You to envelop those memories in Your Holy Spirit, where You put things into perspective and remove the sting and assault against my conscience.

Forgive me for my indulgences and the lack of awareness of the Truth that would have set me free. I forgive all those who did things that destroyed my innocence and who thought it was okay to foist their own shame upon me. As I forgive these ones, I ask that You restore the innocence in my sight—make my eyes new again, as if they had never been defiled, either by my own volition or that of another.

Holy Spirit, I invite you into all my places of pain, to gather every tear that I have ever shed when my heart was traumatized by rejection, abandonment, abuse, violence, or hurtful words. Father, wash away the words that I heard, that came out of my own mouth when I agreed with my accusers, abusers, or those that did not have my best interests at heart. As I forgive them, I also forgive myself. I choose to let myself off the hook and forgive myself for putting things in my line of vision that I should have never seen, and for replaying every offense taken in through my eyes, over and over again.

Forgive me for the contempt that my eyes could not hide and how it penetrated those that I love, as well as those who were my enemies. Jesus, sanctify my eyes afresh, wash away my shame and remind me again that You have never turned Your eyes away from — that nothing ever caught You off-guard or surprised You. Remind me how much You love me and how even the darkest parts of my humanity were light to You. Remind me again that You never broke eye contact with me even when I thought You were not there.

It was me who backed away from You because I was terrified to look back at You — pupil to pupil, because I felt so much like hiding — casting my eyes downward to avoid what my shame told me would be disapproval. Look me in the eyes again and let Your gaze penetrate every moment from the time I turned away because shame came gushing up in my heart. Fill every gap that I missed as if I never missed a beat.

Holy Spirit, I invite you to invade all that my heart has remembered of trauma, loss, disappointment, and failure. Lord, my heart has been like a hard drive picking up fragments of pain in every arena of my life. Many of these fragments I am not aware of, and I cannot access without Your help. I choose not to engage in painful introspection that would not produce good fruit. But rather I submit to You and ask that only that which You want to attend to in this moment would come present to me. I give You permission, like David, to probe my inner-most being and "cleanse me with hyssop and I will be pure; wash me and I will be whiter than snow...Create in me a pure heart, O God, Renew a resolute spirit within me" (*New English Translation*, Ps. 51: 7, 10). I command my spirit to take the driver's seat and all that is in my soul and body yield to my spirit. I thank you, Lord, that I am not on a hunt and seek mission where my heart is concerned, but You highlight in every moment, present continuous, all that needs to be restored and redeemed. I trust You and the finished work of the Cross to pursue me in every place, granting me the Grace to examine my heart and to do that which I cannot on my own.

Next, I invite you into my sexuality. In every place that I have defiled another or been defiled because of my sinful choices, I ask you to wash me anew, removing every trace and residue of sin. I ask you for the grace of self-acceptance and I repent for allowing pornography, any other form of sexualized media, and the false affirmations of others to be the grid through which I saw myself. I renounce the false self and every part of me that abdicated my Heavenly design and perception of who I really am and chose to cling to the creature (others) rather than the One who made me. I received the worship of others in their idolatry, and I also worshipped others in my attempts to secure my own identity. It didn't work and I repent. I divorce myself from every unholy soul tie in the Name of Jesus, and I command every part of me that was given to another to be fully integrated with my true self. Any part of me that I lost, I reclaim it and come out of any agreement with another person who sought to possess me, intentionally or not.

Finally, I ask you to bless my feet, Lord. My feet were created to be the bearers of the Good News of Jesus Christ and I am an image-bearer, an ambassador of heaven. I repent for my many travels into the den of iniquity. I call my feet and my journey blessed.

I declare over myself the words of Prov. 16:9, "The heart of man plans his way, but the Lord establishes his steps." "...He has made my feet like deer's feet, And has me walk on my high places" (*The New American Standard Bible*, 2020, Hab. 3:19). I thank you, Lord, for the journey ahead of me. You have good plans to prosper me and give me a hopeful future (Jer. 29:11).

DAY 26

Revolution of Love

'"Each time he said, 'My grace is all you need. My power works best in weakness." So now I am glad to boast about my weaknesses so that the power of Christ can work through me.'

-*NLT*, 2 Cor. 12:9

But the LORD said to Samuel, "Do not consider his appearance or his height, for I have rejected him. The LORD does not look at the things people look at. People look at the outward appearance, but the LORD looks at the heart."

-*NIV*, 1 Sam. 16:7

God doesn't think as we do. It's a really good thing, right?! God takes the least, the lowest—that which is foolish in the eyes of most, that which looks weak and lame, that which makes no rational sense, and that which has been cast aside or thrown away—and chooses THEM to display His Glory through, while confounding our minds and revealing our hearts. Every generation is easily written off, disparaged, ridiculed, scoffed at, and hyper-analyzed with the fine-tooth comb of judgment by the one that preceded them. And that isn't always without cause, if you just look through a natural lens. In the 1950s, teachers reported that their most prominent issues with students were gum chewing and excessive talking.

Most teachers today would "kill" for such a class.
A few years ago, during a Code Red campus lock-down, the students in my class crouched down, huddled in a heap behind my desk with the lights off in the room—the protocol for a dangerous visitor on campus. In the hush and dim light, I heard their mutterings and gasps of surprise as they beckoned me and each other to see a video of the principal taking down a potential shooter on campus. While we were hiding for protection, we viewed the incident as texts to peers and parents started to fly. Thankfully, the "shooter" didn't have a gun on this particular day but was highly suspect.

Juxtaposed to gum chewing and classroom chatter, we live in a radically different day. Today, the generation is more broken, addicted, angry, sexually confused, lawless, and bankrupt in their identities than previous generations. However, the same God that saved people in the preceding generations still plucks us out of the clutches of hell with His long arm of redemption. He still leaves the 99 and finds the one.

As sin and worldly chaos have progressively increased, the current generation of teachers join the mantra of the generations that precede this one and echo the same complaints and criticisms in every teacher's lounge around the country. Generation-shaming is a timeless cycle. I can listen to teachers all day long talk about the generation's flaws in graphic, belabored detail.

Our "future" is always at risk (and there is truth to that—not because they were flawed coming out of the womb, but partially because we handed them a mess and didn't take responsibility to use our voices and take a stand). They are also partially at risk because of the perceived generational deficiencies that the elder generation projects onto the fledgling one rising up. We project onto them from our sea of regret in a feeble attempt to relieve our sense of shame and failure. For the same reason, parents often live vicariously through their children, mantling them with the burden of our course corrections. We want them to be and do that which we could not. Consequently, we fail to be the harbingers of the righteous revolution that is the heart-cry of every image-bearer on the planet. And that keeps the cycle going.

Because we are created in the image of our Maker, we, too, long to be unveiled and liberated from enslavement to the limits of our humanity. We are supernatural beings made to live, move, and have our being in the spirit (Acts 17:28). Our most authentic and highest potential can only be attained through our oneness with the One who is without limits or restriction.

As Paul says in Romans 8, "I am convinced that any suffering we endure is less than nothing compared to the magnitude of glory that is about to be unveiled within us. The entire universe is standing on tiptoe, yearning to see the unveiling of God's glorious sons and daughters!" (*TPT*, Rom. 8:18-19).

As we embrace the generation coming up behind us, our challenge is to remember that in this era of the church defined by life in the spirit without measure, we are a walking "open heaven," a walking revival, a glory dispenser. As revivalists raising manifest sons and daughters of God, there is a manifold grace in this era to move the unmovable and see the God of the impossible do what we cannot. Simply put, revival transforms and transfigures everything.

The most hardened soul, the most sexually perverse, the most lawless, and the most contemptible humans on the planet are ONE ENCOUNTER away from being transfigured by Love. As we release ourselves from shame's stranglehold in our lives and step into our True Selves, we are freed from projecting onto the younger generation. Instead, we will call forth the gold in them while catapulting them into their promised futures and destinies in the Kingdom of God. The whole earth is yearning to see the glorious sons and daughters emerge on the scene, and we hold the keys.

Pray this with me:

Jesus, I look to You alone as the One who heals me and takes away my shame. Your still, small Voice is as big to me as Your Voice thundering in the mountains. As I navigate the world's chaos, Your Voice tethers me to the reality of the Unseen Real. What I cannot see is more real than what I am looking at right now. Father, I know perception is everything. Heal my myopic vision and bring the revelation that opens the eyes of my heart to the reality of who You are. I seek Your face, not what You're holding in Your hands. I declare that You are a good, good Father and that I am not moved by what my circumstances dictate. I am moved by Your Spirit and every breath You breathe, every Word that comes out of Your mouth. I declare that I do not have to understand everything to trust the One who crafted me in His image and whose very Breath gives me Life. I just turn my face to You and open my heart to hear what You say to me. You have the words of eternal life and I look to You and You alone!

DAY 27

The Restoration of Men and Women

Now the serpent was more crafty than any of the wild animals the Lord God had made. He said to the woman, "Did God really say, 'You must not eat from any tree in the garden?'" The woman said to the serpent, "We may eat fruit from the trees in the garden, but God did say, 'You must not eat fruit from the tree that is in the middle of the garden, and you must not touch it, or you will die.'" "You will not certainly die," the serpent said to the woman. "For God knows that when you eat from it your eyes will be opened, and you will be like God, knowing good and evil."

-NIV, GEN. 3:1-4

I married the love of my life almost 25 years ago at the time of writing. After a painful and devastating divorce, I was overwhelmed at the goodness of God and His redemption in bringing me the most beautiful, powerful, faith-filled woman I have ever known. From the moment I met her at a pastor's luncheon that both my pastor and best friend made sure I attended, I knew I would marry her.

I had vowed that I would never marry again, and that vow was radically interrupted when I saw her come into the room. It only took one conversation for me to realize that we were cut from the same spiritual DNA. It was like we had been tracking in parallel places in our journey up to this point with

169

a few simple changes in the landscape and we "got" each other without effort.

Fast forward many months later, and we were together at a house church meeting at our pastor's home. We sat down to a typical fellowship meal. We knew all the players around the table but one, a man passing through town who knew our pastor and stopped by for a visit. He had a ministry of some sort and took the opportunity of a captive audience to establish himself as a spiritual authority. As a leader and one who had facilitated many similar meetings, I saw someone posturing authority in an inappropriate way given he had no relationship with most of the group and was not there to lead the meeting. When he finished his spiel, my soon-to-be wife, Jane, lightly countered him, offering another opinion. I watched his face redden and knew he didn't approve. Later we were all in the living room and suddenly, shattering the atmosphere of peace, he bore a hole into me with rage in his eyes and blurted, "She's a Jezebel, and you can't marry her! You will regret it, I can assure you, and I would advise you to get out and run from this…" He lost me at "Jezebel," and suddenly I was on my feet, finger brandished like a sword in his face as my unfiltered response came flying out, "You don't even know us! How dare you think that you can come in here and call my future wife a Jezebel!" I looked at Jane, who was radically caught off guard by my very poignant and fiery reaction, and said, "Come on! We are outta here!"

We promptly left, rattled and flustered but chuckling nervously. Now in all honesty, Jane would've been able to handle him just fine all by herself, but I just couldn't help myself because it was so outrageous. We were about to get in the car when I heard my best friend yelling, "Wait!" I thought, "Oh no, he's coming to give me a lecture about my obnoxious behavior." These words followed his beaming smile, "That was incredible!" Arrested in my tracks, I said, "What do you mean, incredible?" "Someone needed to shut that man down," he said, "and you certainly did!" My friend proceeded to congratulate me and told me, even though there were many mouths gaping open in surprise, it needed to get done no matter how messy it looked. Messy it was. I sobered slightly at the thought of the impact my raw response might have had on the rest of the room.

Ironically, I am the guy who is usually supremely gracious and diplomatic. I can read a room, and the pastoral part of me is sensitive to people as well as the Holy Spirit. That wasn't my typical way of functioning. But that stranger's statement epitomizes the depth of misogyny that exists in our culture today. My reaction, messy or not, was a righteous anger at the profound dismissal, degradation, and contempt of women in the culture at large and too often more so in Christian culture.

Prophetically, Jesus is removing the sword between the sexes, the product of the Fall of Man, and restoring honor to both men and women. He is restoring honor where dishonor has been perpetuated in our brokenness throughout the generations.

As fellow image-bearers who God created to become one in marriage as power allies, healing one gender empowers and facilitates healing in the opposite gender. The enmity between women and men inherent in the Fall is irrevocably reversed at the Cross as we apprehend all that Jesus purchased for us. The account of the curse in Genesis 3 aptly identifies the key strongholds and vulnerabilities that have historically plagued men and women alike. Living in the shadows of the vulnerabilities in any form mitigates against the absolute freedom and liberty that Jesus has provided for us.

Our wounds have predisposed us to look for meaning, approval and identity from the created rather than the Creator. In other words, we look to other people rather than our Heavenly Dad, in whose image we are made, to tell us who we are. What was the enemy really taunting Eve with in the Garden? He initiates his taunt by posing a question, "Did God really say...?" He plays on her insecurity and creates doubt, proposing that God is withholding from her a more transcendent reality than what she already had, that she could become like God, not realizing that she already was like Him as His child. He introduces doubt to make her question herself and follows up with that accusation that SHE IS NOT ENOUGH.

The inherent vulnerability in women because of the Fall is that they will battle with insecurity and will be yoked to a man whose power she will crave, but it will be out of her reach as the man in his brokenness will seek to rule over her. Additionally, a woman's children will be a constant source of pain, not only in childbirth but throughout their lives.

Men jokingly like to assume that when God says, "Your desire will be for your husband" (Gen. 3:16) that she will be slightly less than a nymphomaniac. Wrong. God is saying (*my paraphrase*) that men will be tempted to dominate and control women, and women will be tempted to use manipulation in an attempt to take control and power back from him. Men will be threatened, resorting to the power of an assumed position to rule her, and women will lust for their position. At the beginning, they were both commissioned to rule and have dominion together. After the Fall, it became a big power grab.

But when Jesus canceled the curse on the cross, He also established a new order — one of love, honor and co-reigning as power allies. The stranger at the house church meeting accused my wife-to-be of being a Jezebel because she dared to have a thought of her own and, even more so, that she dared to counter him, however lightly, as his equal. Oh, how we have misunderstood the meaning of authority and submission!!!

What does the Curse of the Fall predispose in men? They will live in opposition to women, seeking to find their identity in their work. In doing so, they will perpetually find themselves captive to the futility of the grind of work devoid of the elusive reward that promises to affirm their existence through their accomplishments. When their ability to penetrate their world is thwarted, men often struggle with their identity and find themselves paralyzed by fear.

The good of the masculine is in their ability to initiate, shape, and form, but these attributes are no substitute for intimacy, which is the gold standard for relationships. Adam was equally present in the Garden with Eve when the serpent approached her. In his failure to initiate, protect or intervene, he failed as a power ally to Eve. Later, his shame for his paralysis is highlighted as he blames Eve for their corporate sin.

In perpetuating this dysfunction, many marriages can be like two ticks on a dog with no dog. We are looking for the other to define us, give us meaning and purpose, and to affirm us. Yes, we are designed to experience intimacy and fulfillment in the context of marriage. Still, for us to mutually reap the full benefits of being power allies together with our spouses in marriage, we must gaze upward to our Maker and find our completion in Him.

When we are one with our Creator, we are free to love, bless, and empower our spouse. We do not look to them to define us or tell us who we are. Secured in the love and affirmation of our Heavenly Father, we are freed to love unconditionally. We are no longer in reaction to the opposite sex as one who feels threatened, but instead, we are free to submit to one another in love.

Jesus rendered the curse at the Fall inoperative, extinct, null, and void, as He became the TOTAL embodiment of the curse, paying for it in His broken body. In doing so, He has freed us as men and women not to be defined by our vulnerabilities, predispositions, or woundedness.

The culture of the Kingdom of God is a culture of honor. Everything in His Kingdom functions in the context of honor. Honor is about assigning value to people, finding the gold in them, and mining it, bringing it out. The Holy Spirit is really the One who does the mining and refining. Honor isn't a false humanistic entitlement. It is recognizing the worth of those God created and seeing them the way He sees. It looks past the rough edges, the sin, the mess, and sees what God is redeeming, calling forth, blessing, and wanting to restore. It's a broad concept with broad implications. It means we become the conduit that God anoints to break every yoke, heal every wound, and restore the blueprint of Heaven on the earth.

As we look to God to meet our every need and to restore our souls, we become aware of the limitless nature of the Kingdom of God to transform us and enable us to give away what we have received freely. It redefines our relationships and empowers us to not live from places of insecurity that hinder our ability to love rightly.

It means that men are powerful, and they play a role in the healing of women as they honor what God honors in them, bless them and break off all that has dishonored them. It means that women are powerful in their ability to honor men, bless them, and free them to love. It means that God created men and women as power allies as they are both one (as exemplified in marriage) while still unique in their gender.

At the end of the day, it is all about love. Jesus paid the price for men and women to lay down their weapons of control and manipulation in the power struggle. He made the way for the sword between the sexes to be removed. He has freed us to no longer drink from broken cisterns of sexuality run amuck in our attempts to meet the legitimate needs for affirmation and love illegitimately through an image on the screen or a sordid affair. We were made for Love, and Jesus is committed to transforming us into conduits of that love in every arena of life.

Men, pray this with me:

Lord, I surrender my "doing," my futile attempts to find life in what I do. I declare that I am not the sum total of my successes, jobs, or tangible accomplishments. Unplug me, Jesus, from the "Matrix" of this world of the worship of mammon. I come out of agreement with any place where I have elevated or participated in the empty competition of trying to outdo my peers, bosses, or any other man. Forgive me for any ways that I have sought to control women and hold them down out of my own insecurities. I seek first Your Kingdom, Lord, and I ask you to re-prioritize my life. Like Jesus, I only want to do what the Father is doing. I surrender all my plans to build my own kingdom and legacy and I give myself afresh to You. Teach me, Lord, how to simply "be." I want all that I initiate on earth to be the product of the secret place with You.

Lord, I need You to do in my heart what I cannot. Search me and know my thoughts and the inner workings of my soul. Dismantle and heal every broken part of me and teach me to yield to love. Wash away the shame of my failures, and change my perception of failure. Free me to love others rightly. I desire to be a father in Your kingdom — one that is immune from feeling threatened by those around me, one that promotes others above myself. I repent for comparing myself to other men in all the ways I am tempted to do. I agree with Your Word that I am "fearfully and wonderfully made" (Psalm 139), and I am lacking nothing. Father, affirm my soul as you did with Your Son at His baptism — that I would know that I am loved, complete, and whole as I am. I lay down trying to get it right — trying to manage my life. I want Your life flowing through me. I want to love freely without looking for payment or reward. Make me a walking manifestation of Your Glory on the earth —

a manifest son who knows who I am in relation to You and is free to love, bless, and promote others freely. In Jesus' Name, I pray.

Women, pray this with me:

Jesus, I submit the war against me as a woman to You. Every place that I have been devalued, defiled, hurt, traumatized, disregarded, and discarded by others, I lay at Your feet. I acknowledge before you, Lord, that some of these wounds run deeper than any inner healing, deliverance, or prayer session have been able to touch and heal. I need You to do what I cannot in my heart. I come out of agreement with bitterness and any inner vow that I have made to protect myself from being hurt. I call upon you as my Champion and Father to cleanse me from every wound that blocks the free-flowing fountain of love that You want to gush from me in a present, continuous way. One gaze from Your eyes, Jesus, can heal this broken heart of mine. I come out of every agreement with the lie that as a woman, I lack power and strength or must hide under the shadow of a man to be approved in Your Kingdom. I cut myself free from every entanglement with men who failed to honor me or who were incapable of loving me rightly.

I bless those who have cursed me and attempted to eradicate or enslave me out of their own insecurity. I bless them with the gift of repentance and ask they would encounter You and come to know true freedom. Lord, I ask that you wash away all shame in the places where I have sinned or been sinned against and that You would call me forth into my destiny. Like Mary, I say, "...let it be to me according to Your word" (ESV, Luke 1:38). You are the Living Word. I am Your handmaiden, Jesus, and You are the Lover of my soul. Let Your love complete me in such a way that frees me to love others and myself rightly, without fear and insecurity, in Jesus' Name.

DAY 28

Freedom from Regret

---

*"I admit that I haven't yet acquired the absolute
fullness that I'm pursuing, but I run with passion
into his abundance so that I may reach the purpose
for which Christ Jesus laid hold of me to make me
his own. I don't depend on my own strength to
accomplish this; however, I do have one compelling
focus: I forget all of the past as I fasten my heart to
the future instead. I run straight for the divine
invitation of reaching the heavenly goal and
gaining the victory-prize through the anointing of
Jesus."*

-*TPT*, Phil. 3:12-14

Perpetual regret is often a deep-seated, self-contemptuous
defense. It is typically rooted in an early rejection
exacerbated by subsequent rejections and an irrepressible
expectation of disappointment. Like most self-protective
defenses against pain, regret is a reaction to something that
happened early in life. We are often subtly, or sometimes not so
subtly, living in reaction to our perceived failures and the
disappointments that bombard us in this life, seeking to find a
place at the table of our hearts.

The enemy of our souls finds a seat at that table when
unhealed wounds fester. He desires to destroy us from within,
and he uses circumstances, negative events, even sickness, as
an opportunity to tether us to shame and pull us into agreement

with the familiar lies that have besieged our hearts. As we have discussed throughout this devotional, shame is the deep pain that we feel because of rejection and abandonment that leaves us feeling unwanted and unloved. Regret falls under that broad category of shame.

More specifically, regret is a form of grief that comes because of the death or loss of something that we expected or a dream that is never fully realized when life goes a different direction. In other words, regret is the grief we feel for what didn't happen or what went badly. Guilt and shame in various forms are often inexorably intertwined with regret and cannot always be easily separated. When our legitimate longings for good outcomes in our relationships, work, church and family are thwarted and interrupted by our own perceived failures, the hurt and betrayal of others against us, or by a change in circumstance out of our control, there is grief and loss. We must come out of agreement with the wreckage and torment of the past for us to be healed. We have to be willing to let go of the regret.

Fifteen years ago, my wife and I left the land of our destruction. It was the place where the perfect storm of the enemy came, and for roughly a ten-year period, we were pummeled by injustice, betrayal, and loss. We lost jobs, a business, relationships, homes, land, and more. Christians didn't know what to do with us because our lives were confounding and messy.

We have been in the land of our resurrection for 15 years now, but several months ago (at the time of writing), I had to go back to the land of our destruction to move my parents. On one of the days that I was moving all the hodgepodge that was unpackable at the end of the move, the Lord told me to go by the last house that we owned and to lay hands on it and release it. This custom-built home was by far my favorite—my dream home. Every time I visited my parents, I would finagle a way to drive by, see the house, and lament. Strangely, ever since we foreclosed on that house 15 years ago, no one has lived in it for long. The house had been empty more than it had been occupied. When I went to lay hands on it that day, I was faced with what had symbolized the crashing of a dream, the desires of my heart, and I realized that there was still a soul tie to the house. I hadn't ever been able to fully let it go.

As I was standing there, laying hands on this tangible piece of my soul, I was so keenly aware of my Father's love for me, how He saw me. I could feel His Presence surrounding me. I was overwhelmed with how He felt the pain of my loss. There was something unfinished here that needed to be resolved—for my sake and the sake of wife as well as whoever else would come to occupy the house. It was time to move forward and embrace the new things He had in store.

I felt loved at that moment as it dawned on me that Heaven kept an account of all that we lost, and it meant something to Jesus because it meant something to me. But for me to come into the landscape that He has prepared for us in this new era, He needed me to come out of agreement with the losses of the past season and put them where they belonged—in His broken body.

So, before I left the city where the enemy had effectively leveled us, I released not only the city but the relationships and assets that were stolen or destroyed during that time. I came out of agreement with every regret that had tied me up in knots every time I came to visit my parents. I forgave my various captors, those who played a part in our dismantling in that torrid season of our lives.

As image-bearers, we carry the same Kingdom DNA as

Jesus. He exacted justice for all in His death and resurrection. Sin demands a blood sacrifice to adjudicate Heaven's justice. Regret is the grief born out of our attempt to exact the justice of Heaven ourselves. When the outcome that seems just in our eyes (perception is everything) is not fully realized, and we perceive that God or another failed to act on our behalf, we will exact justice upon ourselves as our contempt is turned inward. Ultimately, we hold ourselves captive to self-inflicted retribution for what we experience as aborted justice. Regret marries well to the shame and rejection we experience when our actions or actions of others thwart our greatest longings for love, acceptance, and affirmation.

Our perceptions, the lies we believe — not necessarily the intentions of others — are paramount in accessing the healing that we need. Jesus delivers us from the "hell of self" as He enters into our greatest disappointments and regrets. In His presence, He beckons us to stand upright in Him as ones who are redeemed from the curse of self-contempt. He ignites hope in our hearts as he realigns us with His purpose, plan, and destiny, assuring us that we have missed absolutely nothing. All that Heaven has intended for us, every page in our book of life that has yet to be fully lived, is not lost as long as we're breathing. We have to assure our hearts that no good thing has He withheld from us. Ever.

Listening to His Voice, we are defined anew as He speaks His healing word to us. We are no longer the ones who missed the boat, but instead, we step into His immersible Grace that comes with the guarantee that we can't mess this up. He is committed to launching us into our destiny more than we are committed to being launched, and He is moving all of Heaven and Earth to bring us into the place we were destined for, regardless of the path we took to get there. That's what redemption looks like in an era of acceleration and time redeemed. The latter glory of the house is greater than the former, and we are the "house." Failure is inconceivable in the Kingdom. We are heirs to a promise, and He delivers us from the tyranny of having to "get it right" to earn it. Again and again, He does for us that which we cannot when we just come into agreement with Him.

Pray this with me:

Jesus, forgive me for ever believing, in any part of me, that Your sacrifice was not enough for me. I come out of agreement with my commitment to punish myself to satisfy an equation when You have already given Yourself as the remedy. I give you the grief in my heart for every outcome in my life that brought sadness and disappointment. I need you to do what I cannot, Lord. I need You to deliver me from myself.

I acknowledge that my self-contempt is an idol that serves to usurp and appropriate what You already accomplished on the Cross. I receive the Grace to let myself off the hook in every event, memory, and scenario in the past where I chose punishment over love and slavery over freedom. I acknowledge the truth that You have not withheld anything from me and that the best is yet to come. I am where I need to be in my journey with You. I am right on time. You favor me, and I trust You in the unfamiliar, unscripted pages of my Book of Life that are before me. In Jesus's Name.

DAY 29

Sight Restored

"They came to Bethsaida, and some people brought a blind man and begged Jesus to touch him. He took the blind man by the hand and led him outside the village. When he had spit on the man's eyes and put his hands on him, Jesus asked, "Do you see anything?"
He looked up and said, "I see people; they look like trees walking around."
Once more, Jesus put his hands on the man's eyes. Then his eyes were opened, his sight was restored, and he saw everything clearly."

-*TPT*, MARK 8:22-25

When we are thrust headlong into fiery trials over and over again, our biggest challenge is to not retreat into an orphan mentality or turn back to Egypt. Everything our heart believes comes bubbling to the surface in the fiery trial. In the midst of the storm, we may find ourselves in long forgotten but familiar struggles. Addictions we hadn't struggled with for years are suddenly front and center again. Our darkest thoughts become our sole companions, and everything we hear tumbles into that pit of rejection that we thought was "mostly" healed. Yet, through many years of perseverance and the roller coaster of trials by fire, we realize that God is good, no matter what. So, we dig deep in the seeming wilderness seasons of life and carve out that place of intimacy with Jesus.

Through such times, we learn how to find Him when the river of Holy Spirit is gushing forth or when there seemingly is barely a dribble. As He is painfully but steadily cultivating our hearts during those exceedingly long seasons of transition, we know intuitively He is preparing us for a much larger landscape than merely our next promotion. We have prophesied to others for years that God will redeem the time, and that we are coming into an era of great fulfillment marked by a series of suddenlies to finally catapult us into our destiny. We have held onto faith that we would begin doing the thing that we were created for in this holy convergence of the ages.

The many years of preparation in arenas that didn't expressly match the call that burned inside us would not be wasted somehow, because they all played a part in our Grand Destiny. We had come to the threshold of what we believed would be the fulfillment of all the prophetic words that had ever been spoken over us along with the words we felt God had given us. We just knew God was about to do in one year what would usually take ten in this accelerated season that we stood at the precipice of.

Our hearts reverberated with great anticipation because we knew that prophetically our lives were about to change drastically. We would look back in six months or a year and wouldn't even recognize our lives, and our hearts would be so full of wonder that the years of loss and devastation would seemed to have evaporated into an almost intangible waft of memory.

This was going to be our year after so many years of prophetic promise. So many, in fact, that we had to fight a burgeoning cynicism as each January first came and went. The waiting and years of cyclical disappointment faded for a moment, the pang of death and sorrow in our hearts seemed to wane just enough to allow a ray of hope to come in and resurrect again. Finally, as an act of pure Grace, our hearts became convinced that suddenly really was "now". And now really was NOW. Our foreheads were like flint. Our backbones were made of steel, having been mortared in the fires. We KNEW it really was our TIME.

Then, the Detour came, and we spiraled and spiraled, gasping for air, hoping to not indeed drown for good. Hoping that He really did hear our solemn prayer while hoping at the same time that He didn't, we say, "God, if you aren't gonna do it, if you aren't gonna truly launch me into the thing that has been forever in my heart since before the time I was even conceived in my mother's womb, then take me straight to Heaven because I don't want to do this anymore." We don't really want to die, and we're not giving the devil permission to take us out, but we simply cannot live in hope deferred any longer. We don't want to hear one more time that this is the path forerunners take. Sound familiar? Can you relate?

It is in the blazing cauldron of our greatest trials that Jesus burns away the residue of our captivity. Even from the womb where we first experienced rejection, the shame that branded our heart is lifted out like an indelible stain that once resisted every cleaning agent. He gives us a new heart that is impenetrable to the lies we came to believe.

Whereas previously, the Word sown into the soil of our hearts failed to take root, the new soil readily receives the Word and produces a bumper crop. Suffering produces... perseverance, character..., hope. And hope does not put us to shame, because God's love has been poured out into our hearts through the Holy Spirit... (*NIV*, Rom. 5:3-5).

Our perseverance in waiting times is a gift that is rarely perceived as such in the moment because our pain blinds us. Jesus is not going for a temporary fix. Nor has He left us to our devices which would only propel us into religious striving.

Instead, He woos us into a place of Rest, and in this place, His Voice, though still and subtle, reverberates like thunder in every fiber of our being. We don't just "hear" His Word, we become it. The Word, Himself, becomes the leaven in the bread permeating every fiber of our being. We move from hearing to knowing, translating us from the temporal to the eternal as we become the Message.

Through our perseverance, which always looks messy and radically imperfect, He forms Christ in us in such a way that shame and the minions of hell that accompany it can no longer find any room in us. We are ruined, unhinged, and irrevocably changed. In our oneness with Him, we can stand in the middle of the storm knowing who we are, and we walk on water as He bids us to come with our eyes transfixed on Him alone.

In the story of the blind man at Bethsaida, Jesus becomes his sighted guide while he is still in darkness and leads him outside of the city gate where He prays for Him two different times. In this passage, the word for "eyes" is one of the few times in the Bible that uses the Greek word, omma, and can refer to not just physical but spiritual vision. This is significant. Bethsaida was also known for its deep occultic practices.

So, what is Jesus doing here? Like this man, Jesus has to lead us through excruciatingly long seasons of what has felt like darkness. As our sighted guide, He walks arm and arm with us, leading when we cannot see or understand. Finally, He removes us from the place of warfare that has clouded our vision and takes us outside the gate and tells us to "look up." He prays again for our sight to be restored spiritually, and suddenly that which has been obscured becomes crystal clear. The circumstances may not have changed for the blind man as he returns to his home shrouded in constant warfare. But now he can see. Jesus is not removing us from the world or the war, but He is changing how we see. No longer will the blind man come to the trials in his life with the eyes of victimization or be shrouded in shame, feeling abandoned by his Maker. Instead, he will see every trial and challenge as an opportunity for the miraculous, to see the God of the impossible do what he cannot.

Pray this with me:

Jesus, I know the Unseen Real is more real than what I am seeing. Help me to look up and receive healing for my sight. Lord, I know that perspective is everything. I thank You for being my sighted guide in my darkest hours, but I ask You to heal my spiritual sight in such a way that cauterizes my doublemindedness and burns through the residue of unbelief in my heart. Make my vision and heart single. Come and do, Lord, what I cannot. I declare and decree that I no longer see things only as they appear here on earth, but the Unseen Real becomes more real than anything I see in the natural. As one who is bilocated in Heaven and Earth, I ask You to so blur the lines as I walk in both realities that I hardly know which one I am in. Marry heavenly and earthly sight in my heart, forever changing the lens through which I see the world. Father, I submit all my "whys" to You. I don't need to understand those things You have relegated to mystery. I establish on the front end of this new season that I don't have to understand it all or see it all to know that You are Good and that You are with me. Make my new question a "what?" question and not a "why", that I may always see and do what the Father is doing. What are You doing now and how can I partner with You in it? That is the desire of my heart. Amen.

DAY 30

The Father's Blessing

Phillip spoke up, "Lord, show us the Father, and that will be all that we need!"

-*TPT*, JOHN 14:8

My mother remarried when I was 12 years old, and my stepfather, who has been the only father I have ever truly known, adopted me, became my dad, and gave me his name, Infante. Getting a name change through adoption has such spiritual significance. No longer would I be identified by the trauma associated with my given name. One day, in my father's attempt to truly understand my behavior that was a constant source of dismay and trouble in the school system, he asked me a question. "What is the worst thing that has ever happened to you?" Immediately, with uncanny self-awareness as a 12-year-old, I said, "My father leaving when I was five." It dawned on him that the pain of this abandonment was at the very core of my acting out in school. It didn't explain everything, but it did shed light on much.

Many years later, as an adult in my early 40's, I would read a letter from a half-sister that I only knew briefly from a couple of visits I had with my biological father and his wife. The first visit was ironically right after I was adopted. The psychologist I was seeing thought it would be a good idea, so my parents planned the visit.

The second visit was unexpected when I just showed up

at my sister's eighth birthday party after hitchhiking and walking for miles. Earlier that evening, at about 9:00 at night, I was walked off the premises of a drug program facility that I had just been kicked out of. I showed up on the doorstep of my biological father only to find out that he was no longer living there with his wife. She graciously took me in. I was 18 years old and had recently graduated from a high school that I only attended for eight weeks after running away from home. I was a bit of a mess.

In my sister's letter, she told a horrific account of being brutalized by our biological father. Her last memory of him was having her head pounded on the floor and going unconscious as he raged and almost killed her. She was the one who would wipe the blood off the walls after he would beat her mother. My two half-sisters and I shared a common denominator: a biological father who had abused his kids in unfathomable ways. I talked in an earlier chapter about how I forgave him from the heart many years prior in a powerful encounter with the Lord. It was during an inner healing training school session that left me in a fetal position on the floor, wailing myself into exhaustion. At the end of this encounter, a place opened up in my heart that had been walled off years prior. I had relived the abuse of a memory that I carried as a black and white film in my mind since I was two years old. Suddenly, the pain was gone. Sadly, in the letter my sister wrote, she had not come to the same resolve. She continued to live in reaction to the pain, building some pretty significant walls in her heart and trying to find safety in whatever relationship she could forge with another woman. Fatherlessness. Then brokenness. It's a common story.

I have been engaged with youth in the education field for over 20 years. As a high school teacher, I have rarely taught honors or advanced placement students. Instead, I have chosen to teach students with learning and life challenges in my English classes. Most have already had a hard life, ones Jesus goes after that many have kicked to the curb. These are the diamonds in the rough, who desperately need to be called forth into their destiny—even more than to apprehend the literary devices in the classic literature pieces we're supposed to read, as good as that can be. They need to be told who they really are in the Kingdom, not the story their tattered and torn history told on multiple social media platforms. They already knew that story. What they long to hear is who they are and what they were created for. They need a father, and that's what I am to them first and foremost. Secondly, I am their teacher. If they know they are loved first, whatever we need to deliver in the classroom to satisfy the gods of the system would become much easier from that place of relationship, not just to earn a grade.

For the past few years, the seniors I have taught are a lot like me. Lost. Many were fatherless. Some fathers were incarcerated. Some they have never known. Some they have known and sadly have become part of their trauma. Some were lost in work and were absent by default. Thankfully, some have present fathers who can affirm and bless to one degree or another, but this is increasingly rare. In this era of fluid sexuality, trans-everything, and family compositions that are more diverse today than in any previous time in history, fatherlessness is the single most common denominator.

There is a hopelessness that can be seen in many of my students' eyes, some who have lost more family members through homicide and incarceration than you can imagine. Rage masks the hopelessness and despair that they feel, and the concept of believing in a promised future is a pipe dream or someone else's life story. The shame of never knowing a father's blessing runs deep to the core. Because children are egocentric, the only interpretation for a child when a father has gone rogue is that something must be deeply and irrevocably wrong with them that he could not want or love them.

There is no reparenting for any of us in this life in the most literal sense. But, as Phillip aptly articulated in John 14, "Lord, show us the Father, and that will be all that we need!" The only One who can meet the needs of a fatherless generation is the Father Himself. Jesus became our example at His baptism of what a father's love looks like. "Then suddenly the voice of the Father shouted from the sky, saying, "This is my Son — the Beloved! My greatest delight is in him" (*TPT*, Matt. 3:17). The Father's affirmation of Jesus came before He "did" anything. This same affirmation frees abandoned sons and daughters from the slavery of religion and the temptation to heal their own rejection through futile attempts to earn the love their hearts crave. The Holy Spirit inhabits our weakness by lavishly pouring into our hearts the Spirit of Adoption by which we cry, "Abba! Father!" (Rom. 8:15).

In a generation that feels so radically forgotten, forsaken, and discarded, Jesus will inhabit their weakness — making them the most prolific generation of lovers the world has ever known. They will penetrate the earth, carrying the goods of the Kingdom as Manifest Sons and Daughters who have been baptized by Spirit of Adoption.

As ones who know what it means to be anchored by the Father's love, they will carry revival and not squander what Father has so lavishly bestowed upon them. They will be a stark contrast to previous generations who faltered under the weight of the anointing because their souls were unhealed. This generation will not know fear or unbelief because they will know The Father's Blessing, and unlike Philip who didn't fully realize Who had been in front of him the whole time, they will comprehend that they have everything they need because they have encountered the Father through Jesus Christ (John 14:8). I am prophesying life to this generation—to you! Come to the Father and live!!

I release a father's blessing over you in this final prayer in the devotional. I am modeling a couple of things here. First, any manifest son or daughter of God can release a parental blessing over those who have great deprivations in the arena of parental love. Secondly, you don't have to be totally healed or have it all together to be a conduit of blessing. You simply must be willing. If we were to wait until we thought we epitomized what it means to be a father or mother in the faith, we simply wouldn't do anything. Thirdly, you can give away what you have not received in the natural because you are connected— you are one—with the One who has it all. So, as I release this blessing over you, I pray that the Voice of Father Himself will encounter you, that He would inhabit this prayer of faith and draw you into the fold of His Love which reconciles all things.

Father's Blessing:

Holy Spirit, come and pour out Your Spirit of Adoption on your son or daughter. As a father and conduit, I release the Father's Blessing over you and into you. I call your spirit to the front, with soul and body aligned behind, and I release healing for your soul into every wound that has been sown into your heart by an earthly father, including the wound of rejection and abandonment. Father, let Your love go into every time and dimension — past, present, and future — and enter into every place of hurt and loss. Let your son or daughter feel the warmth of Your presence, even now, descending upon them and moving through every part of their body. I declare that every aspect of your spirit, soul and body is good. You are fearfully and wonderfully made and lack nothing. I release the grace for self-acceptance, that you will finally feel at home in your skin — that you will see yourself as your Father sees you.

I release healing to your eyes to set you free from every distorted image of maleness or femaleness that has come into your conscious and unconscious mind. The water of redemption and healing now washes over you. I release the grace to come out of agreement with every image that runs contrary to who you really are and that obstructs your ability to see yourself rightly. I release your spirit, soul and body from every trauma that the enemy used to assault your psyche, your physical being, or your perception of self.

I break every unhealthy soul tie in the Name of Jesus with every individual you have been connected to that perpetuated the wounds in your heart and played a part in defiling you, with or without your permission.

I declare over you that you are healed and no longer an orphan — no longer a victim to being defined by the sins you have committed or those committed against you. You are free—washed clean of every residue of defilement, rejection, abandonment, and trauma.

I declare over you that you are fearfully and wonderfully made and that you have a promised future and destiny. All the days of your life have been written in your Book of Life (Psalm 139). I ask the Holy Spirit to break open the yet-unrealized destiny chapters and set you ablaze with holy purpose. I declare that you will never doubt the calling and the gifts that the Father has placed in you from this day forward. You are now walking forward into your destiny, and no enemy will be able to keep you from apprehending your calling or moving in the gifts that are resident in you by the power of the Holy Spirit.

I release a father's affirmation that assures your heart that you are loved, wanted, and the apple of your Father's eye. I release love where fear has once ruled and declare that you are now walking in the love of a Father with your heart secured in Him. I unleash in you a resoluteness and passion that will never die or fade. You will burn brighter and brighter as you rise up into the extravagant love of your Father.

As one who is fully loved, affirmed, and secured, you will freely give away all you have received. I declare that you will not be intimidated by any man or woman but will boldly embrace all that He has for you.

Your Father in Heaven is more invested than you are in seeing you walk in your destiny as a manifest son or daughter. Therefore, I declare that you can't miss it or mess up anything that He has prepared for you. He just needs your agreement, so go ahead and say yes to Him.

Finally, I ask that in every high and low moment you encounter from this point forward, one truth will remain—you are loved. Nothing can separate you from His love, and your union with Him will be your safe haven and solace in time of need. I declare that you are a walking manifestation of His Glory and that you are putting a demand on Heaven, releasing the Kingdom inside of you, as you enter the harvest fields He has prepared — for at such a time as this.

Afterword

In writing this devotional on shame, I was surprised at how many triggers of my own, anchored in shame, have resurfaced in the process. It felt like the enemy unleashed an unholy avalanche of junk on me, flooding my soul with a reminder of every previous struggle I have experienced — struggles I thought I had permanently dealt with. Through this mental and emotional assault, I realized that Jesus is going after every residue of shame and self-contempt still lingering in the recesses of my heart like fragments on a computer hard drive. Eventually, these fragments of data must be consolidated and removed for the hard drive to be quick and healthy.

It's not that I haven't previously been healed and set free. It's a continual process as we walk in this fallen world, with new things attempting to convince us to accept the badge of shame again. So, Jesus was using the topic I was engaging with to defragment the hard drive of my soul. I accepted this process again as part of what it meant to take a deep dive into the exploration of shame and its impact on the soul for this book project.

In a contemplative moment with Jesus, I submitted my sanctified imagination and waited to see what He would show me or say to me. It is the practice of His Presence in this manner that gives Jesus free reign to override my defenses and encounter me in an unexpected and transformational way.

Immediately, I saw Jesus hanging naked on the Cross. I was horrified and knocked sideways by the idea of Him being naked — which was the way that the Romans crucified their criminals. I know that in my head as a historical fact. It's just not the way I would ever have pictured Him.

His genitals were at my head level and, without

thinking, I turned around to face away from Him, backing my head as close as I could to block His humiliating exposure to the many witnesses present. I felt like I was there to buffer His public shame. So, I didn't expect what came next out of His mouth. He said, "Scott, you don't have to do that." "But Lord", I blurted, "I don't want the world to see You this way!" He said, "You must. I AM humiliated—naked and exposed in every way—so that you can be covered in My glory and honor. I took your shame in My own naked body so you could be set free from shame. In my public disgrace, your self-acceptance is made secure."

There wasn't any further dialogue, but I "knew" that He was paying the price for me—for all of us!—so we can feel at home, without shame, in our own skin. Every bit of guilt, insecurity and shame generated from my own sin and those committed against me was atoned for in His naked body and through His public humiliation. He paid for me to be fully clothed in Him—in the union that He and I share together.

My prayer for you, at the conclusion of this 30-day journey, is that you will walk in the freedom that Jesus has provided—that you, too, will be free from shame.

Freedom on steroids!!

Doc Scott

About the Author

Dr. Scott Infante (also known as Doc Scott) has been married to the love of his life, Jane, for 25 years. He is a father of four and is also a grandfather. He is an educator, pastor, revivalist and prophetic forerunner.

He has over 30 years of experience in many realms of public education and pastoral ministry. This unique blend of educator and pastor has enabled him to forge deep relationships in the rising generations over decades. His expertise has been forged on the front lines of the education system as a bold Kingdom carrier. He has seen God do incredible things (physical and emotional healing, salvation and more) in the context of the public-school arena and in the community as he has ministered to adolescents and adults.

Doc Scott earned his doctorate at Trevecca Nazarene University. In his doctoral studies, he explored a topic that was extremely relevant for the times in which we are living in a dissertation entitled, "A Systematic Review of the Physiological, Psychological, and Spiritual Impact of Pornography in Males." He has aptly noted that this current generation is the "most pornified generation that has ever existed." Pornography is writing the behavioral scripts for how the generation functions in their sexuality, and this is a powerful contributor to the sexual fluidity of the day. We are migrating exponentially from the blueprint of Heaven for our relational design as image-bearers. The generation at large is in crisis — an identity crisis of epic proportions that is rooted in trauma and shame.

Doc Scott has a passion to see the fallow ground of shame in the heart of the believer broken up, liberating sons and daughters of the Kingdom to receive the love they long for and to be lovers of Jesus with unveiled faces—a mirrored reflection of the One who made them and in whose presence they become all that they were created to be in the earth.

To learn more, please visit Doc Scott on Facebook at—

Doc Scott Infante

To sign up for the 30-Day course that includes 30 companion videos and audio podcasts for each day, go to **www.30dayChainBreakers.com**.

Made in the USA
Columbia, SC
28 January 2024

30496115R00117